This call for professionalism is timely. At a time when the investment management industry's business model is being challenged, John provides a clear and understandable set of recommendations for advisors as to how they should serve clients to help them secure better options for their savings and retirement income security.

—Ed Waitzer, partner, Stikeman Elliott LLP, and former chair of the Ontario Securities Commission

The advice in *The Professional Financial Advisor IV* provides the reader with much-needed insight into the financial industry. John carefully explains the biases of financial advisors and empowers the reader with the ability to ask the questions necessary to protect their investments while understanding the financial planning process. Essential guidance for all Canadians!

—Kelley Keehn, media personality, author, and personal finance educator

The business of giving financial advice is in the midst of significant change due to a combination of changing client expectations, regulations, and technology. John paints a forward-looking portrait of how to navigate an industry in transition. This book is required reading.

—Atul Tiwari, chairman of the Canadian ETF Association and managing director, principal, and head of Vanguard Investments Canada Inc.

A manifesto for putting clients first. John De Goey could be the best friend investors have in the advisory business.

—Rob Carrick, personal finance columnist, *The Globe and Mail*

John De Goey has distinguished himself as a steadfast advocate for higher standards governing the investment advisor and dealer community. He has been fearless in confronting industry pushback against much-needed reforms, and calling out that opposition for what it is. Canadian investors have benefitted greatly from John's principled and uncompromising views. It's truly great to know there are people like him within the investment industry, striving to turn it into a profession.

—Neil Gross, former executive director, FAIR Canada

John knows his stuff. He understands the conflicts in the industry, and has structured his business to avoid the pitfalls inherent of the industry. John cares for his clients, too. Focusing on proven, low-cost strategies, John is definitely a bit of an outlier compared with the typical advisor in Canada, but we need more like him.

—Peter Hodson, CEO of 5i Research Inc. and editor-in-chief of *Canadian MoneySaver* magazine

The Professional
Financial Advisor IV

Putting Transparency and Integrity First

John J. DeGoey

Library and Archives Canada Cataloguing in Publication

De Goey, John J., 1963-
[Professional financial advisor]
The professional financial advisor IV / John J. De Goey. –
[Fourth edition]

Revision of: De Goey, John J., 1963-. The professional financial advisor.
Issued in print and electronic formats.
ISBN 978-1-55483-173-9 (paperback).--ISBN 978-1-55483-178-4 (PDF)

1. Financial planners--Canada. 2. Investment advisors--Canada.
3. Financial services industry--Canada. I. Title. II. Title:
Professional financial advisor

HG179.5.D44 2016   332.6'20971   C2016-906855-2
C2016-906856-0

Printed and bound in Canada

Insomniac Press
520 Princess Avenue, London, Ontario, Canada, N6B 2B8
www.insomniacpress.com

Disclaimer

The opinions expressed are those of the author solely. The opinions and generalizations by the author concerning professionalism within the financial services industry reflect the lack of homogeneity among numerous providers of financial services from differing industries (insurance, banking, financial planning, and investment) and with differing standards of conduct. For advisors who are regulated by the Investment Industry Regulatory Organization of Canada (IIROC), some of these generalizations about professionalism are not accurate.

With respect to opinions relating to modern portfolio theory and passive versus active management, an attempt has been made to discuss these complex academic issues in simple terms. As such, the discussion does not fully reflect the breadth and depth of opinion and evidence regarding these topics, nor can it be expected to. Everyone's investment and retirement plans must be created to satisfy their particular situation. Therefore, it is recommended that the reader treat the information in this book as general in nature and consider getting advice from lawyers, accountants, financial planners, and other related professionals.

For Marina

CONTENTS

FOREWORD BY PREET BANERJEE

Within a few months of entering the financial services industry, I felt uneasy. I remember the day the unease started, too. I was in a corporate training room, along with about twenty or so other would-be financial advisors. During a break, we were discussing our scores on the licensing test required to sell mutual funds and required for us to be in this particular training program. One person proudly exclaimed that he had scored exactly 60%, which was a relief to him, as the minimum score required was, you guessed it, 60%. Most of the people listening seemed sympathetic, vicariously relieved on his behalf. He said he felt lucky.

My first thought was somewhat contrarian to the tone of the room: I felt sorry for the future clients who would end up with an advisor who only barely met the minimum requirement to pass an exam that takes roughly two weeks to study for.

Fast forward a few years, and I had started opining about the industry on a blog, frequently engaging financial writers of all stripes. I had written a book of my own, a credibility-building exercise, and had shopped it around to said financial writers, hoping for a crumb of exposure. And exposure I did receive.

One writer with a prominent national newspaper asked for an interview to talk about the book. I eagerly obliged, of course. After what I surmised was the end of the formal interview, the writer in question asked me what I thought was an off-the-cuff question, to which I provided an off-the-cuff answer. I was on the inside now. We were pals. We were bonding.

Q: So what kind of mutual funds do you recommend for clients these days?

A: The evidence suggests focusing on asset allocation, and as cheaply as possible, so I just use index funds and focus on the financial planning. That's the true "alpha" an advisor brings to the table.

The question and answer are paraphrased—this exchange occurred almost ten years ago—but what I can quote verbatim is the headline that appeared in that prominent national newspaper: "New breed of advisors shun mutual funds." Not exactly what I was expecting from an interview about a book on forty-one different RRSP tax rules and strategies.

That day, my phone started ringing off the hook with a relatively even distribution of prospective clients and calls for my head from within the industry. It was probably one of the most significant forks in my life. On one hand, I was fearful for my career. On the other hand, there was a clear demand from financial consumers for something different from the status quo.

A few months later, I was at an industry event when a tall suit read my name badge and, with widened eyes, reminded me that I was "that guy from that article." At that point, I had developed something akin to a fight-or-flight response whenever someone brought up the article. They were going to either berate me or celebrate me. Nothing in between. Luckily, the tall suit fell into the latter category. He said, "My name is John De Goey, and you and I need stick together."

I recognized his name. Whatever roller coasters I had been on as a result of having a public, divisive opinion, John had ridden them before me. I had read his op-eds and his letters to the editors of various trade publications. I remember feeling self-doubt about my opinions, and having those doubts weakened or eliminated by reading the thoughts of someone like-minded.

John is still an advisor, but I am not. That initial unease I felt about the industry never really left me, and although I'm no longer a practicing advisor, I comment frequently on personal finance issues in various media. As a result, I'm constantly inundated with requests for advice, and I've lost track of how many times people have asked me to "come out of retirement" or if I could work under a special arrangement. It's flattering, and telling at the same time. It's telling of the pervasive skepticism of financial consumers.

Some suggest that financial advice is just a few ingredients away from being a true profession, but I suggest an alternative hypothesis: The industry is only just now starting to see changes that will start to take us away from a predominantly sales-based culture.

Indeed, John and I have "stuck together" in the

sense that we regularly chat about the industry's ongoing evolution. Ultimately, we both believe that an informed consumer can make informed choices. Reading John's book will bring you a long way down this path.

Preet Banerjee, September 2016
Author, personal finance commentator, and *Globe and Mail* columnist

My website, www.preetbanerjee.com, has a full conflict-of-interest disclosure section, but relevant to this discussion is that I currently consult for several financial institutions that have financial products and services to sell, and I have received speaking fees from financial services companies on numerous occasions. They still hire me even though I may not always say things the industry likes. I believe this is because more and more people within the industry see the inevitability of the change that is slowly coming.

A MESSAGE FROM JOHN DE GOEY

This book, like its predecessors, has been designed to open and foster a discussion about professionalism and also to identify existing failings in both the system and the observed practices among some participants. Dialogue is positive and constructive, and a level playing field makes for the best dialogue.

To that end, I feel compelled to express some frustration. I am a registered portfolio manager with the Investment Industry Regulatory Association of Canada (IIROC). As such, I am governed by the rules of IIROC when I publish into the public domain, most notably under IIROC Rule 29.7 (1). I am also governed by the *Conduct and Practices Handbook* (*CPH*) for IIROC-approved persons. The latter contains the code of ethics for investment professionals and a detailed manual for acceptable professional conduct. These are good things. These are the very core pillars of professionalism that are discussed in this book. I not only support them; I make it my personal goal to foster them industry-wide.

That said, when I publish within the limits of these rules and the code of professional conduct, I am at a disadvantage compared to those who hold conflicting views and yet have no similar limitations. Taking IIROC Rule 29.7 (1) as an example, it requires (among other things, as this is not an exhaustive list) a prohibition against the publication of material that

- contains an untrue statement, or an omission that is misleading;
- uses unrepresentative statistics to suggest unwarranted or exaggerated conclusions;
- contains any opinion not clearly labelled as such; or
- is detrimental to the interests of the public, the regulator or the firm for which the author is employed.

In short, the onus is on me to publish material with assertions that I can prove are true, with no omissions that could make the material misleading, with statistics that are representative and draw no exaggerated conclusions, and with a clear distinction between facts and my opinions. This is an admirable and professional standard. As a professional, I do not object to these rules in the slightest, but I do object when other commentators are not held to the same standard.

In my opinion, not all those who participate in the conversation about professionalism are held to the same standard of academic and professional integrity. Generally, I would say that certain detractors of the premises in this book have not been held to such a high standard. One example of my desire to provide balance and clarity is the copious use of phrases such as "in my opinion" and "the way I see it" in this book. There are likely well over a hundred such caveats found within these pages. Although I could have added more, I've made every reasonable effort to express reasoned, evidence-based opinions so that the reader can distinguish between verified evidence and personal opinions—without compromising readability.

I'd like to thank my proofreaders, Marina Magagna, Mark Magagna, John "Jazz" Szabo, and Mario Frankovich, for their enormous assistance in making this book more user-friendly. Their input has been invaluable. Every edition of *The Professional Financial Advisor* has acted as a bridge between advisors and consumers. Compared to previous editions, however, in this edition, I very deliberately included fewer acronyms, plainer language, and more charts, graphs, and images so that I could convey the sometimes complex concepts of my industry quickly and intuitively. I really hope you enjoy this new approach.

John J. De Goey, September 2016

PART 1

SETTING THE STAGE

CHAPTER 1
WHY DOES PROFESSIONALISM MATTER?

Some time ago, I coined the acronym STANDUP (Scientific Testing and Necessary Disclosure Underpin Professionalism), a term that intuitively captures both where the industry was headed (due to forward-looking advisors) and where the industry needed to go (in spite of slow-moving legislators and regulators). It is both inspirational and aspirational, intending to draw out the best in people. Slowly but surely, a STANDUP way of doing business has been rising to prominence in Canada. What we need now is for those remaining advisors who have resisted positive change to stand up to the financial services establishment and to stand up for their clients' best interests. This evolution has been happening for years already, but now the modest trickle has become a mighty river.

It seems that some people have only belatedly come to realize that transparency and the primacy of client interests and old-fashioned integrity matter a great deal. Of course, there have always been those who would say that genuine professionalism should come first, no matter what the field of endeavour.

Today's financial advisors need to demonstrate in clear terms that they are working for their clients, not their product suppliers or employers. That is the primary concern of virtually all debate about retail financial advice today. The specifics of exactly what advisors do can come later. There is little doubt that consumers are increasingly becoming aware of the conflicts that many financial advisors face and that there are many considerations that might cause advisors to stray from their clients' best interests. Once primary loyalty has been established, one can safely assume that other elements of good advice are sure to follow. The client-centred, evidence-based, "do what is right" approach is something that goes to the core of all advisory relationships.

Some advisory activities are generally accepted as having considerable value in the marketplace, while others are simply attributes of a STANDUP value proposition. For instance, what exactly is the value of coaching someone to save just a little bit more from every paycheque?

In addition, the word *advisor* is really just a blanket term that means "someone with a licence to sell a financial product." There are three main types of licences: one to sell insurance, one to sell mutual funds, and one to sell securities. Some advisors have more than one licence and so can sell any of several different product types. There are two additional little wrinkles that you also need to know about. The first is that some people hold designations that demonstrate a specialized capacity in the field of finance. The specialty designations could be in financial planning (e.g., CFP, or Certified Financial Planner), portfolio management (e.g., CFA, or Chartered Financial Analyst), or specialized underwriting (e.g., CLU, or Chartered Life Underwriter). This is by no means an exhaustive list. Pretty much everyone who is an advisor has a licence, but only a segment of those advisors have additional designations, sometimes called accreditations. The second is that some people have an accreditation or two but no licence to sell things.

Ironically, the unlicensed people often refer to themselves as advisors, although they are more precisely referred to as fee-for-service or fee-only advisors because they have no legal capacity to sell you any investment products, only their own services. The challenge in the financial services industry has long been in helping ordinary consumers get good advice and to be confident that the advice they are getting is reasonable, appropriate, and without a conflict of interest. Virtually everything in the pages that follow applies to advisors who are licenced to sell things. In some specific instances, however, we'll delve into the details of how to regulate those who have certain accreditations.

Here's where some people get confused. It's a bit like functions and relations in high school math class. Some advisors have a licence to sell things and an ac-creditation. Others (the fee-only type) have only an accreditation and no licence. Most advisors have a licence (or two) but no accreditation. In the pages that follow, the word *advisor* refers to anyone who is licenced to sell investment-related products, irrespective of which licence it is or whether they have any accreditations in addition.

At a minimum, it now looks as though some people with accreditations might soon achieve full professional status (i.e., something that is entrenched in law). Looking a little further down the road, it seems reasonable that all advisors at some point might be fully regulated and granted professional status. This casting of a larger, more inclusive net will likely take many more years. Still, we have to start somewhere, and the people who are both licenced to sell products and accredited with additional specializations will likely be the first to attain full professional status. Others will likely follow over time.

This book will challenge the long-held assumptions of many readers. The intent is to look at the current situation using logic, common sense, and the best, most reliable information on the subject. We'll discuss the appropriateness of how advisors become advisors, the ongoing debate about the "efficiency" of capital markets, the impact of product cost, the role of the media, the role of psychology, and, perhaps most tellingly, the role of the primary business models in determining the attitudes held by advisors today.

In the final section of the book, we'll look at what governments and regulators (both in Canada and abroad) have been doing in light of considerable evidence that the current system is flawed. We'll also look at what individual consumers can do to ensure they are engaged in a fair, purposeful, professional relationship with their advisor. This includes a few questions that investors might want to ask their advisor to ensure they'll get straight answers. Near the end of the book are some phone numbers for those who want to advocate for more change.

The time to act is now.

What Do STANDUP Advisors Do?

Over the past decade or so, we have seen a voluntary shift within the advisory community. Many have voluntarily moved to be more client-centred. That trend is likely not only to continue but to accelerate. Look at it this way: A physician who stubbornly refuses to use new procedures or medicines is considered unprofessional. Blatant refusal to stay current can lead to malpractice suits. Physicians are required to protect the health and welfare of their patients, and full professional disclosure is simply a part of how true professionals conduct their affairs. Similarly, it would be difficult for any advisor to be considered a true professional if the advice they offered did not incorporate the fullest breadth of products, services, and evidence currently available.

Working with a STANDUP Advisor

A whole raft of services that were once considered value-added is now being given away as financial information becomes commoditized. In the twenty-first century, technology has seen to it that people can easily bypass advisory middlemen. Meanwhile, the need for wisdom, context, strategic thinking, and client focus is as great as ever. As times change, the things that were once considered essential to add value have become severely devalued. If good financial advice is not synonymous with stock picking (or its first cousin, fund picking), then what exactly is it that reputable advisors do to earn their compensation? Ironically, it's pretty much the opposite of what most people think.

Let's begin by taking a quick look at some of the things traditional advisors used to do. These services included providing stock quotes, offering a consolidated statement of holdings, researching proprietary securities, and executing trades. Do you notice anything about this list? Anyone who has access to the Internet now has access to all of these services. All of them are absolutely free, save for trade execution, which is almost free. Any advisor who provides only the services listed here is an advisor whose day in the sun is essentially over.

Let's take a step back. There is little doubt that advisors moving with the times need to be absolutely clear about their true role. Having established what it is not, it stands to reason that many people have some useful ideas about what that role should be. One such person is Dan Wheeler, a retired industry veteran, who said:

The role of the advisor is really a defensive role. The advisor is there to manage expectations, to make sure that all the bad things that can happen to people and their capital do not happen—things like market timing and tactical asset allocation. If you're moving money in and out based upon some type of economic forecast, you endanger the person getting the capital market rate of return and getting to the point where they want to be years down the road.[1]

If Wheeler is right, what can STANDUP advisors help with and what additional activities might a consumer want to consider?

Ongoing Coaching

It needs to be noted that offering good financial advice is not a one-time event. Instead, financial advice is an ongoing process of coaching and prodding that evolves as life takes shape. People graduate from school, find work, get married, start families, pay off debts, take on mortgages, get promotions, endure disabilities, buy second properties, suffer temporary setbacks, and experience myriad other things. Life happens.

Consumers need to be able to change with the times in managing the various developments in their lives, and advisors should enable their clients to focus on all aspects of their financial lives, with the most important things being addressed first. This requires strategic direction. Some form of financial planning is recommended at the beginning of a relationship in order to establish priorities and to sketch out a course of action. In some instances, there isn't a formal plan, just a brief discussion focused on narrow investment matters and perhaps the provision of insurance. In fact, some commentators are fond of saying that if most financial advisors were charged with financial planning as a crime, they would be exonerated because there wouldn't be enough evidence in their files to support the charges.

Until recently, advisors have been able to "hold out" using dozens of different titles. That is part of the problem. It should come as no surprise that consumers are confused when regulators allow advisors to choose from a list of literally dozens of potential titles, often with no express subject matter expertise to support the title. Advisors should all be engaging their clients in regular, consistent, predictable processes and procedures to make sure they are on track with their financial goals.

There are many ways they can achieve this. For example, clients can work with their advisors to complete self-diagnostic checklists on a wide variety of financial matters including general financial awareness and aptitude, investment planning, debt management, tax planning, estate planning, disability and income protection, and asset protection. A qualified advisor has a pivotal role to play and, in many instances, will likely add value to the relationship. Of course, since financial advice is not free, consumers should consider what they're getting in return for their money.

This value determination is often a challenge because consumers can have perverse ideas of what good advisors do. Many resent paying their advisor if they have lost 10%, even if markets lost 20%! Conversely, many don't mind paying their advisor if their portfolio has gone up by 10%, even if markets have gone up by 20%. Both attitudes are conspicuously and dangerously focused on simple investment outcomes, often in the short term. A more appropriate approach might be to look at portfolio performance relative to life goals, accepting that some years will be better or worse than others. Some commentators have suggested that there are really only three important attributes that advisors should have. They should be able to

1. spot problems and identify solutions;
2. motivate people to act/change their behaviour; and
3. emotionally detach the client from investment markets.

Although this is a clear and simple synopsis of what advisors can (and probably should) do, it should also be stressed that they probably should not be doing any of the other things that many consumers and media pundits seem to think they should be doing. In short, the role of a STANDUP advisor is to help consumers navigate the emotional minefield of financial decision-making.

How Can Advisors Add Value?

Perhaps the easiest description of the function of an advisor is "to assist investors in overcoming their own irrationality." Advisors can also add real value through simplification. Clients benefit from advisors who simplify and enhance their lives by doing the spadework of filtering data, developing shortlists, calculating adjusted cost bases, securing T3s and T5s, interacting with other professionals, or simply coaching them to top up that RRSP. Putting an accurate price on it is virtually impossible, but it would be hard to deny that these activities are worth something to most people. A true STANDUP advisor works as a sounding board for virtually all financial matters. Proper orientation includes focusing on the following:

- Diversifying both within and throughout asset classes
- Aiming to capture something close to asset class returns
- Being cost sensitive
- Understanding and explaining risk/return trade-offs
- Focusing on clients, not markets

In contrast, some traditional advisors may emphasize some of the following:

- Picking stocks and/or mutual funds
- Trying to time the market
- Focusing primarily on investment returns
- Focusing on investment products, not actual clients

Financial Planning

One thing that will almost certainly become clearer in the near future is the use of the term *financial planner*. Of all the terms and titles in the industry, there is likely none that is more misunderstood and misused. Many people use the term as if it were a synonym for *financial advisor* or sometimes *mutual fund representative*. In fact, these are two separate things. Financial planning is an unregulated profession. Having demonstrated a specific financial planning skill set is not a precondition for using the term. In English Canada, there is currently nothing prohibiting anyone from calling themselves a financial planner. This is the case even though there is a dominant and clearly understood international designation for financial planning: Certified Financial Planner (CFP). In terms of demonstrated capacity, in-Jonathanvestors should look for the CFP mark if they want financial planning. Even if someone refers to themselves as a financial planner, that term means little if the letters "CFP" do not appear after that person's name.

It now seems likely that that last bit is about to change. Led by the Wynne government in Ontario, legislators are finally beginning to put some actual meat on the bones of who can use the term *financial planner*. Rules will require people to demonstrate proficiency in financial planning. The test in using the term and applying the concepts should be straightforward and simple, and it seems that accredited financial planners (e.g., CFPs) will likely be the first subset of people calling themselves advisors to achieve legislated professional status. According to the most reputable financial planning organizations worldwide, including the Financial Planning Standards Council (FPSC) in Canada, there is a clear six-step process to financial planning:

1. Understand the client's situation.
2. Clarify goals and objectives.
3. Identify any particular barriers or unique circumstances.
4. Make written recommendations with clear alternatives.
5. Implement the chosen route.
6. Review the plan regularly.

Most people reading this book will not have the tools to purposefully implement all the required aspects of a comprehensive financial plan, many of which require specialized knowledge. A comprehensive questionnaire that goes into great depth on matters of tax and estate planning, business succession, proper use of insurance, and advanced financial planning solutions should be required. To make the most of qualified financial advice, the person offering the advice needs to be completely thorough in practicing their craft. These other planning-oriented skills are often more specialized and therefore more valuable, although many people might not need that level of advice if their situation is straightforward.

Finally, consumers should remember that financial independence projections are made using assumptions only, but these assumptions need to be reasonable at all times. If it turns out that someone falls short in their financial independence projections, only four possible assumptions can be altered:

1. Savings rate: Clients could save more of their income either monthly or annually—many cannot.
2. Rate of return: Returns are fairly predictable provided one takes a longer view—most assumptions are far too high.
3. Retirement date: Waiting longer increases savings and delays depletion—most people should consider retiring later if at all possible.
4. Reducing lifestyle in retirement: This should be considered only as a last resort.

All things considered, STANDUP advisors can play many vital roles. As educators, they can teach clients how to frame their expectations. As coaches, they can help them retain a proper focus. As financial physicians, they can work to find the best treatment available based on investment science. Along with these important roles come important challenges, such as convincing clients that their own brain often misleads them and keeping investors calm when markets are choppy.

When I talk to friends who have moved up the corporate ladder and into management, many say their biggest challenge is managing people. They don't know the half of it. Dedicated and enlightened advisors have to manage people who are often irrational, emotional, and unaware of their own biases in dealing with their life savings! This occurs against the backdrop of the popular media constantly acting as though unimportant things are actually extremely important.

When offering advice to clients, I believe people should focus on what they can control (influence) rather than what is on their mind (mere concerns). Management requires control, and woe to the advisor who takes responsibility for something they have no control over. The obvious example is that we may be concerned about performance, but we can't reliably control it. Meanwhile, we can all control things such as our savings rate, product costs, portfolio turnover (leading to tax bills), and, to some extent at least, our own behaviour. In short, there are many things a STANDUP advisor can do to assist people in arranging their financial affairs, but they have almost nothing to do with stock picking, fund picking, or market timing.

CHAPTER 2
BECOMING AN ADVISOR

To paraphrase Pogo: "We have seen the enemy, and he is us." As much as the financial services industry likes to portray itself as being on the cutting edge, the dominant culture is deeply conservative and resistant to change. To better appreciate the business of giving financial advice to retail consumers, we need to look at how the business has changed over the past thirty years or so. As we will see, many of the challenges of the past generation are still around today despite the protests to the contrary.

Where Did We Come From?

Until the late 1980s, the dominant model for retail investor portfolio design was one of working with a stockbroker, mutual fund representative, or insurance agent who earned commissions while constructing a portfolio of individual securities or selling insurance products. Clients paid commissions for the buying and selling that occurred as a result of that advice. On the investment side, people really had no choice but to work through full-service brokers or mutual fund representatives because discount brokerages were just coming into existence.

The problem with a transaction-oriented business model is that it rewards all transactions—good, bad, or otherwise. Anyone who has seen the movie *The Wolf of Wall Street* can understand the potential abuses. More trades meant more commissions for the broker, and that was simply a cost of doing business.

More recently, many people switched from investing in individual securities to investing in mutual funds as personal finance became democratized through a growing middle class in much of the West. Recently, many of those original investors have since switched again, this time to exchange-traded funds (ETFs). Many of these people, however, still do not know exactly how products like mutual funds and ETFs work, what they cost, or how advisors are compensated. In general, the industry has moved from giving away the advice while charging for the transaction to virtually giving away the transaction while charging for the associated advice. In this age of having information at your fingertips, and the answer to almost anything being only a Google search or Siri inquiry away, the only viable value proposition that advisors can offer is superior advising. Knowledge is knowing that a tomato is a fruit; wisdom is knowing not to put it in a fruit salad. Good advisors need to demonstrate wisdom.

Attitudes Constrain Progress

Some people reading this might be thinking that giving financial advice is already a profession. Not surprisingly, that's what people in the industry would have us believe. Many refer to themselves as "trusted advisors" since offering trusted advice seems like an entirely professional thing to do. The time has come to check for accountability. Are advisors really delivering the things they claim they do? Furthermore, how can consumers determine whether their advisor is, in fact, doing a good job?

As someone who has spent nearly a quarter century working as an advisor, I can assure you that advisors don't always deliver what they claim to. Although there are many excellent advisors, there are also advisors who not only fail to add value but may well actually subtract value. In fact, it is entirely possible that there is no field of endeavour where the range of expertise, skill sets, and activities is more varied than in the field of giving financial advice to retail consumers.

To get a sense of what I'm driving at, note that old course materials used to refer to advisors as "sales agents," and, frankly, that's what they were. Today, there's an ongoing and accelerating transition that recognizes that the best advisors are far more comprehensive and useful than mere sales representatives. There are some old-school advisors who have not kept up. Until very recently, corporate infrastructure and incentive frameworks encouraged these old-school advisors through their focus on product sales.

There are still many areas where old and new remain in conflict, but there is a clear trend toward purposeful progress. The following factors will drive the change:

1. Statutory requirements and professional standards
    Every profession has its own association for individual practitioners, and several industry trade associations have sprung up, vetting the professional standards and competencies of individual advisors. Many traditional professions self-regulate. There is growing talk that financial advisors will soon be regulated in one way or another. The primary issues are: Who will do the regulation and what will the regulation entail? Note that this might be done by product licensing, by proficiency certification (e.g., for financial planning), or by some combination of the two. As an example, today, the Investment Industry Regulatory Association of Canada (IIROC) licences and sets proficiency requirements for securities advisors and also sets a code of ethics through a conduct and practices handbook.

    This is surely the clearest evidence of a young profession. There is already a broad consensus on the general attributes of what constitutes a profession, but also there is a whole lot of backbiting about who will monitor those attributes and protect consumers along the way.

2. Accreditations and designations

How are consumers going to determine which credentials are most appropriate if the financial services industry can't even agree amongst its own practitioners? When people go to see a physician, they expect to see a medical degree and other official documents displayed prominently in the office, attesting to the fact that the person they are seeing is an MD qualified and licensed to practice medicine. The same goes for dentistry, accounting, engineering, and architecture. Professions hold themselves to a consistent standard as set by consistent and rigorous training, suitable experience, peer review, and ethical conduct. This in turn gives consumers a degree of confidence about a minimum level of competence. There is no such standard regarding financial advice in English Canada.

There are currently over a dozen designations available to advisors who want to demonstrate competency in some field of financial advice. Many people in the financial planning community feel the fragmented situation is outright embarrassing. What self-respecting profession can't even agree on what is required to join? Today, the industry is coalescing around the Certified Financial Planner (CFP) designation conferred in Canada by the Financial Planning Standards Council (FPSC) as the title that most accurately denotes an advisor who can offer qualified advice to the public. This doesn't mean the other designations are substandard, only that they often convey competence in a more specialized area. The FPSC mandate is to "benefit the public and the financial planning profession by establishing and enforcing uniform professional standards for financial planners."

If holding a designation were a precondition of working in the business, we would have fewer (perhaps substantially fewer) practitioners. In a world where consumers hope to seek out true professionals throughout the country, people holding out as practitioners need to make the scope of necessary knowledge available in towns throughout the countryside as well as in the big urban centres. Everyone knows what to expect when seeking out a medical professional, but when they're scarce and the nearest one is a two-hour drive away from where you live, then ready access and highly personalized medical care wouldn't likely be considered part of the offering.

3 . Unbundling

Unbundling (the removal of embedded compensation) allows for investment products that clients can consider based on merit and suitability alone. There will be no second-guessing an advisor's motive. Clients would no longer have to wonder if their advisor is recommending a product because it's best or simply because it offers more compensation. It is doubtful that true product independence could ever be attained without unbundling.

The financial services industry has already gone through a partial transformation. It has become widely accepted that charging using a predetermined fee schedule based on household assets under management is likely a better way to eliminate compensation-related bias. Ironically, this might involve clients' paying an advisor to do nothing. Remember, however, that doing nothing (e.g., deliberately not trading) is frequently the right thing to do. Where that is the case, people should hail this as significant progress.

The aim here is to develop a framework where the advisor's motive (and corresponding advice) is aligned with client interests. We have to get to the point where an advisor's motive cannot reasonably be called into question. We need standardization so that compensation considerations are no longer allowed to cloud the issue of product suitability.

Embedded commissions cause advisor bias, and advisor bias creates a conflict of interests that flies in the face of everything that professionalism stands for. The continued availability of embedded compensation products is especially disappointing for do-it-yourself (DIY) investors who want to use advances in technology to engage in "disintermediation." These people often end up paying their discount broker for the (non-existent) "advice" costs that are built into certain products.

Many advisors want to be thought of as full professionals in the minds of consumers. They position themselves as professionals who can wisely discern suitable options in a sea of complicated financial choices, but their business models sometimes undermine that trust. The best advisors know that without trust, advisors can say whatever they want and their clients still won't likely believe it, even if what they say is measured, appropriate, and fundamentally true. There is a clear need to suspend self-interest when offering financial advice, and unbundling does this. There's a certain kind of unimpeachable integrity that comes from being able to say, "There are a few options here; the pros and cons of each are as follows, and no matter what you choose, I'll be paid the same. The best option is the one that works best for you."

An honourable goal for any advisor is to create an environment where the truth can be spoken, heard, and believed. There will almost certainly be a premium placed on good governance and transparent business relationships. Many advisors have already moved to unbundled relationships voluntarily.

Where Consumers Fit In

There is a wide range of consumer demand for financial services in the marketplace, and it is often difficult for advisors and their firms to deliver a consistent "brand experience" when consumer wants and needs are all over the map. Some consumers want more detail on statements, while others would be quite content to get fewer statements altogether since they often don't open them anyway and generally see reporting as a nuisance. Part of the problem is that some consumers find statements too difficult to understand.

When considering the different types of consumers of financial products, we can draw a continuum that demonstrates the problem. On one extreme, we have people who want to do everything themselves and find any contact with the financial services industry a nuisance; on the other extreme, we have people who do virtually nothing for themselves, choosing instead to abdicate their responsibilities altogether. Both extremes can be dangerous. The continuum looks like this:

More Involved			Less Involved
<———>			
Do-It-Yourselfers	Collaborators	Delegators	Abdicators

Most consumers find themselves somewhere in the middle and are generally inclined to some degree of collaboration, with an increasing likelihood of working with an advisor as they move to the right. The challenge for advisors is that many are trying to be all things to all people, working with whoever comes through the door. The more an investor moves rightward, the greater the likelihood of needing an advisor. Advisors would likely be better off if they focused on one subset of the population: the delegators. Delegators at least have a moderate sense of ownership and involvement.

Complete abdicators might want to consider working with a discretionary advisor or risk the possibility of nothing getting done due to their own unwillingness to even look at statements in some instances. Note that abdicators are even more likely to do as they are advised, but they generally don't make for fulfilling client relationships. When advisors offer stewardship to clients who appreciate it, everyone feels more fulfilled. Rendering advice is more rewarding when there's a sense that the people receiving the advice really want to take destiny in their own hands rather than be prescribed generic solutions.

John Heinzl, an investment reporter and financial columnist for *The Globe and Mail*, agrees. He told me:

I strongly encourage people to learn as much as they can about investing, whether they work with an advisor or use a self-directed account. Fortunately, investors today are asking more questions about things like costs, compensation, product suitability, and such than ever before. Seeing as they also have so much good information available to them, they should be able to find and apply whatever knowledge they need fairly easily.[2]

There's no single best way to determine whether or not one should work with an advisor, but many people will need one at some point in their life. The important thing is to both know yourself and feel assured that your advisor is properly trained and prepared to work on your behalf by focusing on your circumstances and goals along with you.

What sort of preparation do you suppose we're talking about?

CHAPTER 3

PREPARING ADVISORS

There can be little doubt that we are in the final stages of the creation of a new profession. People have been giving financial advice for years without it being a true profession, just as people built structures before there were professionally certified engineers. Over time, the need to formally train workers and standardize the construction work being done moved from being good ideas to being entrenched as requirements for doing business.

Since the financial services industry evolved from the notion that advice is a by-product of sales, as opposed to being a necessary precondition of assessing suitability, we've spent entire generations putting the cart (a licence to sell a product) before the horse (the demonstrated skill set to offer value-added advice).

The need for qualified financial advice is especially dire for certain segments of society: professionals, corporate executives, and business owners. These people often lead busy lives and need to consider a wide range of options that take into account a wide variety of variables and possible outcomes. Their multiple objectives may require them to consider trade-offs and make difficult choices. Let's have a look at what some of the more established professions do.

Written Disclosure of Material Risks and Limitations

Physicians and surgeons are among the most revered professionals on the planet. They enjoy a level of implicit trust that most other professionals couldn't even dream about.

Although these medical specialists routinely perform many delicate procedures, they still insist on written disclosure and consent before proceeding. It is standard procedure for them to sit down with the patient and explain, in terms the patient can understand, the risks and limitations of the procedure they are considering. What is the likely outcome for the patient if they do nothing? What is the probability of success? How long is the recovery likely to take if the operation is successful? What is the probability and frequency of failure? What is the worst that can happen? Has the procedure been explained to the patient in clear terms that the patient understands? If yes, has the patient ultimately consented to the procedure?

This is all documented in writing, and the patient will be asked to sign an informed consent waiver form acknowledging these discussions and disclosures before heading to the operating room. The chips will fall where they may, but at least the patient made the decision with a clear and purposeful understanding of what the problem was and what the risks, rewards, and limitations were before getting started. It should be obvious that this process also protects the professional.

The opinion that financial advisors should be obligated to make certain disclosures before their clients can purchase products has gained momentum. Point-of-sale disclosures have recently been introduced on a product-by-product basis. I think we could do better, and I would like to see something that goes further—something that discloses the attributes of competing products with similar mandates. An example of this kind of thing is the EnerGuide sticker found on appliances. That information not only shows you how much energy a particular appliance uses; it also shows you how much energy other appliances use. Perspective is critical. How exactly can people comparison shop if no comparisons are available?

Some advisors recommend products based on superior short-term performance even though there is evidence that short-term performance is not indicative of long-term performance. Over longer time frames, the percentage of products that beat their benchmarks decreases. Not all advisors disclose these points, and few consumers think to ask what might go wrong as well as what might go right.

If a surgeon explains every reasonable facet of a procedure to a patient but does not receive written consent to proceed and something goes wrong, there may be a substantial liability. Why should the standard be any different for someone's financial health?

Itemized Deliverables and Expected Conduct

Unlike other professionals, lawyers seem to get little respect from the general public. There are three things that lawyers do, however, that are extremely professional: they 1) use letters of engagement, 2) have a set fee schedule, and 3) carry liability insurance. Let's take a look at each of these and explore how the use of a similar series of documents would raise the bar substantially for financial advisors who wish to present themselves as professionals.

The Law Society of Upper Canada (a self-regulatory organization for lawyers in Ontario) has taken the unusual step of defining professionalism for its practitioners. It defines professionalism as follows:

> As a personal characteristic, professionalism is revealed in an individual's attitude and approach to his or her occupation, and is commonly characterized by intelligence, integrity, maturity, and thoughtfulness. There is an expectation among lawyers that professionalism will inform a lawyer's work and conduct.

The Law Society goes on to itemize the various components of professionalism. The "building blocks" listed are: scholarship, integrity, honour, leadership, independence, pride, spirit, collegiality, service, and balanced commercialism. The widely accepted concept of professional practice standards is gaining credence everywhere. One of the most important aspects of such standards is the letter of engagement. Here, both the nature and the scope of the engagement between the client and the professional are mutually defined and agreed upon before services are rendered. There are many aspects to this concept, including the following:

- identifying services to be provided
- disclosing both the nature and the amount of re-muneration involved
- identifying the responsibilities of both parties
- establishing the duration of the agreement
- disclosing any related ties or potential conflicts of interest (both real and perceived)
- confirming confidentiality

Financial advisors need to be absolutely clear about how much they charge by using a compensation dis-closure document. A separate disclosure document at the point of sale would go a long way toward clarifying how and how much advisors are paid.

All professionals carry liability insurance to cover errors and omissions. Lawyers deserve some credit because they are perhaps the most keenly aware of the liabilities they assume when offering their services to the public. Clients should have some assurance that they will be covered in the unlikely event of a major oversight or error on the part of their financial advisor. After all, their personal fortune is usually at stake.

Lawyers are self-regulating through the use of law societies. Ontario legislation, primarily the Law Society

Act, authorizes the Law Society to educate and license lawyers and to regulate their conduct and competence. The Law Society's bylaws set the professional and ethical obligations of all members of the profession. Those who fail to meet these obligations are subject to the society's complaints and disciplinary process.

The observation that most people make in reviewing these attributes is that they are positive when present but that they are unenforceable in a world where financial professionals and sales representatives co-exist and where the latter are not held to the same standards as the former. The short answer is to establish clear terms of reference for professional conduct in provincial law so that all advisors are regulated in some fashion.

When competency becomes a clear differentiator, consumers will be able to vote with their feet if they recognize that the person advising them is ill equipped to do so properly. The day may soon come when people will be forced to clearly present themselves as either proud sales representatives or proud professionals.

Perhaps most tellingly, consumers of professional services often choose their professionals based on relationships and the gut feeling they have once they come into contact with them. We're all human, and no one wants to feel like a number or an account or the living embodiment of a certain number of billable hours. There is a saying that virtually every advisor comes to learn within weeks of starting the job: People don't care what you know until they know that you care. Although it's a little trite, it's generally good advice.

Advisors are often reminded that they work in a relationship business in which connecting with the client is more than half the battle. Unfortunately, most consumers don't have the wherewithal to make a meaningful judgment in assessing the services provided by an advisor. They look at the décor of the office, gauge for a suitable firmness of handshake, and hope that the person who referred them did not have a uniquely positive experience before recommending the services of the advisor in question. All the while, the prospective client is thinking, "I sure hope I can trust this guy."

The client has to presume that the advisor has a certain level of competency and a reasonable degree of personal integrity. Conversations are held, goals are explored, and written recommendations are made before most clients embark on a business relationship. As a general rule, the more understanding the advisor seems to be, the more likely they are to get the business. Some would say this represents the triumph of compassion over competency.

Competency combined with compassion is preferred, but given the choice, society has clearly chosen competency over compassion. In the professions, it is better to be a brilliant technician with horrible people skills than a horrible technician with brilliant people skills. Imagine a mediocre student who is known as a nice gal in medical school—someone who everyone likes and who has the most pleasant bedside manner in the class. Even if her grades indicate otherwise, should her professors pass her just so prospective patients can experience her wonderful demeanour?

Many of the most valuable benefits that accrue to those who work with effective advisors are emotional rather than logical or intellectual. How can anyone solve human problems if consideration is given only to non-human questions of dollars, tax rates, income levels, and pension plans? This, by the way, is one of the arguments used against the so-called "robo-advisors" that are just emerging on the scene. In case you are not familiar with the term, robo-advisors offer basic algorithm-based advisory services such as asset allocation and ongoing rebalancing and tax-loss harvesting.

There's so much that many advisors don't know, largely because they haven't been taught. After all, so much of what advisors convey to those they work with is predicated on what they were taught in the first place. Before consumers can become competent in financial matters, advisors need to be competently taught. Otherwise, misinformation, no matter how well intentioned, can take hold and lead to poor planning decisions down the road. Most people giving financial advice today were not formally (i.e., academically) trained to do so.

There's a lot that goes into creating a profession, and we need to consistently address many technical questions before financial advice will become a truly professional calling. These include matters of preference, reasonable assumptions, and disclosure. Some examples might include the following:

Integrating Suitable Investments with Actual Goals

The objective "to retire at age sixty-five in 2027 with no debts and a retirement income that is at least 60% of what I averaged in my last five years on the job and lasting for as long as I live" is seldom found anywhere on a "Know Your Client" application form, unless the advisor writes it in in the comments section. This despite the fact that such a sentence would demonstrate that the client and advisor have mutually and succinctly defined financial independence in personal, measurable, and practical terms. Some see the lack of articulate personal goals on client application forms as a stumbling block to better engagement. The financial services industry is regulated by product choices and their suitability.

Fee Impact on Calculations and Expectations

The need for meaningful disclosure is dire. For instance, what rate of return should be used for financial independence calculations? In the 1990s, some advisors would tell their clients that they should plan to get long-term returns in the neighbourhood of 10% or higher annually. Many of the most highly respected academics expect long-term equity returns to fall within the 4% to 7% range. That's a far cry from the numbers that many advisors often assume when doing financial independence modelling for clients. Furthermore, everyone should plan for retirement based on real return: the return above inflation. After all, you'll be living your retirement (and paying for it) in inflation-adjusted dollars, not today's dollars. Simple logic demonstrates that the average return for any investment is likely to be the return of the benchmark minus the investment's cost.

For example, if the Canadian stock market experiences a long-term return of 7% while a mutual fund investing in that market has a management expense ratio (MER) of 2.4%, the expected long-term return for the investor is 4.6% (the return of the market minus the cost of the product that gives access to that market). Note that this is only 2.6% above inflation. Over the course of twenty or more years, the difference is gargantuan. There are illustrations elsewhere in the book that show this impact using both historical and expected returns.

For those readers not familiar with the term *management expense ratio* (MER), it is the total annual cost of owning a mutual fund. It is applied against your return and deducted silently and automatically. Returns are reported net of MER—after these fees have been deducted. Depending on the type of product you own, part of the MER might be a commission paid to your advisor.

The Financial Planning Standards Council (FPSC) and its Quebec counterpart, Institut Québécois de Planification Financière (IQPF), recently released their joint 2016 recommended return assumptions for various asset classes[3]:

Inflation:	2.1%
Fixed income	4.0%
Canadian equity	6.4%

Foreign developed equity	6.8%
Emerging market equity	7.7%

Advisors who use assumptions that are substantially higher could lead consumers to have unreasonable return expectations. What's more, advisors should not use planning assumptions that do not take MERs into account. That's inexcusable because it implies that cost does not matter when, in fact, cost matters a great deal. To act as though a 10% (after-cost) return is a reasonable return expectation is therefore doubly bad. To begin with, a more suitable pre-cost return might be 7%. With costs of 2.4%, a more suitable expectation might be more like 4.6%. Many advisors tell consumers to expect double-digit returns on equity positions when, in fact, mid single-digit returns are more likely—and low single-digit returns are more likely for balanced portfolios.

Time Diversification

Many advisors encourage investor clients to take "a long-term view." Clients, in turn, often ask their advisors how long "the long term" really is. There's no simple answer. The short answer, however, is that returns become more stable and predictable over time. Short-term experiences can be wildly favourable or moderately terrifying. Long-term experiences trend toward historical averages. There's a saying in the portfolio management business: Returns are unknowable in the short term, but in the long term, they are virtually inevitable. Recent iterations of client application forms are doing a much better job of identifying time horizons for various accounts and ensuring a consistency of purpose and general suitability between what's being held in the account and the clients' objectives.

Process, Not Product

At a minimum, advisors should be able to offer clients a consistent experience. Many advisory firms stress the importance of having a clear, repeatable process in place for all manner of things: opening new accounts, engaging in client discovery, making initial investment recommendations, and offering ongoing advice and reporting. They talk about doing these things using a consistent, repeatable, and unambiguous process that leads to more predictable outcomes.

What Next?

So what do we need to do to ensure a transition to professional status? Most old-school advisors will be retiring in the near future, so let's not be too worried about retraining them. In the eyes of many, the biggest difference between them and the people now entering the business is their training, both in the classroom and in starting out in the industry. Let's take a look at what advisors, both past and present, are taught.

CHAPTER 4
EDUCATION OR INDOCTRINATION?

Personal beliefs are funny things. Creationists and evolutionists are equally adamant that their worldview is right. Agnostics are the Switzerland of the religious world; they don't take sides. In many ways, agnostics are prudent, since neither the creationists nor the evolutionists can offer incontrovertible proof that their view is correct and that the opposing view is conspicuously wrong. Precious few advisors are indifferent to certain viewpoints when it comes to choosing between competing paradigms of portfolio management. This polarization has made it difficult for ordinary investors to get unbiased input regarding their options.

All three licensing options (insurance, mutual funds, and securities) have their educational requirements set by regulators. As a result, the education system is supposed to be formatted based on generic information that pertains to each particular product line. For example, there is no context in any of the courses to compare and contrast the merits and drawbacks of mutual funds versus securities.

More specifically, the Canadian Securities Institute

(CSI) was created in 1970 as an educational institute under the authority of the securities commissions and became fully independent of dealer firms in 2007 when it was purchased by an independent educational organization. Once advisors have completed their exams and are licensed to sell products, however, the training and overall culture of their employers comes into play. The following discussion looks at how certain industry practices might compromise the principles of professionalism.

The Pre-existing Sales Culture

To begin, I'd like to offer a disclaimer: The following passages discuss potential problems that can occur in a sales culture. There are no allegations against specific dealers or their agents in that respect. I am simply pointing out that certain outcomes are more likely in a sales culture than in a pure advisory culture. Since the idea of giving financial advice has grown out of a culture of sales, it stands to reason that there are a number of people giving advice today who were trained more in "closing the sale" than they were in offering comprehensive, holistic, evidence-based advice. As the saying goes, if you're good with a hammer, everything looks like a nail. Accordingly, many advisors who were taught how to get people to open their chequebooks to buy things continue to work as though that were still their primary function—their "value-added" if you will. This raises the following questions:

1. Aren't advisors expected to do what is in their clients' best interests at all times?

2. Shouldn't advisors work to identify the strategies that are the most likely to be successful and then pursue those strategies, perhaps exclusively?

3. Using a medical analogy, if your physician said the odds of success were 70% for one procedure and 95% for another, would you be indifferent regarding the procedure you chose?

4. Should professionals be taught one way of looking at the world or, if the matter in question is contentious and impossible to either verify or deny, should they be taught all the possible explanations of how things work?

How Markets Work

There two predominant views about how markets work. What follows is a simplification, but most people in the industry would likely acknowledge that it is broadly accurate:

1. The traditional view of managing a portfolio is to trade stocks, bonds, and mutual funds in an attempt to beat the market. This is known as "active management," and it assumes that markets are at least somewhat inefficient.

2. The more recent viewpoint is that attempting to beat the market is costly, difficult, and likely to not be worth the time, effort, and money. People who invest with this in mind prefer using a strategy called "passive management," and it assumes markets are highly efficient.

The debate about the utility of each approach has raged for decades, but you'd never know by reading the course material required to sell securities, mutual funds, or insurance. Owing to the massive amount of content required to be conversant with the traditional approach, virtually all licencing courses test would-be advisors to see how well they can explain the bells and whistles of the products (or individual securities) they would be licenced to sell in contrast to being tested on how to give overall integrated advice to the valued clients who would come to them looking for advice.

Who Teaches Advisors?

Only recently has the industry started to come to grips with its own flawed logic. Each industry "silo" features independent institutes testing their candidates, but those tests often fail to offer context. The securities dealers test candidates for knowledge about securities. The mutual fund channel tests candidates for knowledge about mutual funds. The insurance channel tests candidates for knowledge about insurance. All of them have their registrants offer their services as advisors, but none of the registrants are actually trained in *how to give advice* to retail clients to help them with their ongoing, real-life financial problems. Again, you'd need extra training for that. Many get it. Many don't.

In the end, probably less than half of all licenced advisors have any additional training beyond their licence to sell things. As such, it should be obvious that professional status likely shouldn't be conferred to just anyone with a mere licence to sell investment products. As a result of the notion of giving advice as an adjunct to selling a product, virtually all advisor educational training has been conducted by the organizations that grant licences. They are predisposed to portray their products in a favourable light yet are not particularly regimented like a university. The limitations of and the alternatives to the products being tested for are seldom mentioned.

It might be said that the courses that grant licences to sell financial products are predictably focused on the narrow attributes of the products themselves. As a result, course graduates might know a fair bit about stocks, mutual funds, or life insurance but relatively little about the broader context in which these products can be applied. The disciplines of economics, law, public policy, and ethics are not considered vital to getting a licence, but virtually everyone would agree that they're crucial to giving comprehensive advice.

Virtually all advisors working in the industry are effectively self-taught, meaning they bought textbooks, worked through them on their own, and then wrote their exams. Unless advisors take special preparatory courses, there is usually no formal classroom learning going on at all. The Canadian Securities Course (CSC) is jam-packed with information about understanding and interpreting financial statements; everything you'd ever want to know about bonds, preferred shares, common shares, and the factors affecting security prices; and various details about stock exchanges and trading. The same goes for the mutual fund and insurance licencing textbooks, where there's lots of information on products. The emphasis in these varied licencing courses includes the strategies employed by professional money managers on both the macro and micro level: government fiscal and monetary policy, and security valuation techniques. Meanwhile, these textbooks include next to nothing about giving sound advice to retail clients. Registrants present themselves as professionals but are trained—to this day—to be product-centric sales representatives.

What's interesting is that the course content changes only modestly from year to year and is still quite similar to what it was long ago. Could it be that the people setting the licencing exams for our advisors are engaging in a presumptive close of their own? Specifically, how can anyone reasonably expect advisors to offer a fair depiction of the relative merits of active and passive approaches if they have been taught only one of those approaches? When you're good with a hammer....

People tend to believe things based on what they were taught in their formative years. University-level finance textbooks discuss the various strategies and techniques that portfolio managers might employ in attempting to add value by improving risk-adjusted returns (lowering risk, increasing returns, or both). Licencing textbooks barely touch on these things.

What Are Financial Advisors Taught?

Teachers have a massive responsibility because they collectively shape the opinions, attitudes, and competency of their students, who, in turn, are responsible for our future. Students tend to believe much of what they've been taught simply because they trust their teachers. As a result of teachers' presumed expertise, there's an implicit credibility associated with many established teachings, allowing for a certain degree of intellectual imperialism.

When broadly based teaching gives way to more concentrated sales-based training, the perspective that comes from the more formal and often more rigorous approach might be lost. The healthy skepticism that normally comes from a well-rounded university education might well be lacking in the more focused curriculum associated with licencing courses. This might arise through what is implied precisely because it is not taught.

For instance, where are the references in licencing textbooks to the fact that the majority of money managers fail to beat their benchmarks over statistically significant time frames? Evidence to that effect is everywhere for those prepared to be inquisitive and dispassionate, but newly minted securities, mutual fund, and insurance salespeople are essentially not taught about how rare it is for their kind to actually succeed at beating the market. Instead, they are taught about techniques used in the market regardless of potential for success. To my mind, that lack of context is presumptive, and the knowledge that advisors glean from it as a result is at best incomplete and at worst misleading. True professionals would never train new practitioners by withholding relevant information.

Education or Indoctrination?

A simple definition of *indoctrination* might be "teaching people to take your side." Note that this does not mean that your side is either right or wrong; it means that only one side of an issue is being taught.

In universities, students in both the sciences and the humanities are encouraged to take courses that offer competing views of difficult concepts. That way, they will be well equipped to look at information from varying perspectives in order to make informed decisions. This provides a stark contrast to those seeking a licence to sell financial products.

I asked Moshe Milevsky, a highly respected and well-known professor at the Schulich School of Business at York University in Toronto, to offer his thoughts about what is taught to finance students. Here's what he said:

> When finance professors in training are in graduate school, they are continuously fed a steady diet of efficient market theory using the rigour

and language of mathematical economics. And, even though some of the papers and studies they are forced to read contain empirical evidence that violates these assumptions, it is more of the exception than the rule. They graduate to professorship with a very passive view of the world. Then, of course, they come in contact with CFA practitioners and MBA students whose raison d'être is that markets are inefficient and value can be obtained by picking securities. This is why many of the assistant and associate professors of finance you might encounter in graduate school have a schizophrenic attitude to market efficiency and indexing. Some courses might be very dogmatic while others are agnostic about the whole thing.[4]

How can advisors be expected to ensure consumers make purposeful decisions about competing views of a contentious industry matter if they themselves are oblivious to competing alternatives? Some of the most progressive minds in the industry don't even think advisors need to pick a side since there's an argument to be made for both approaches. I tend to agree, but I think that advisors should be able to at least do a decent job of fairly representing both sides if a client asks for a comparison.

The real endgame of independent financial advice might even bring advisors to the point where they are indifferent. Perhaps *indifferent* isn't the most precise word, either. Perhaps *balanced*, *adaptive*, and/or *purposeful* might be better words. This is not so much about who's right and who's wrong. Instead, it is a question of preparation that calls to mind the proper incorporation of concepts such as professionalism, training, informed consent, and the primacy of client interests. Irrespective of what anyone believes personally, if one takes the view that neither side is unequivocally correct, then shouldn't consumers at least be made aware of their options and the evidence in support of each?

Modern Portfolio Theory

If portfolio construction is not about security selection or product knowledge, then what is it about? This brings us to the question of how to best help people construct and manage their portfolios. In the late 1950s, Harry Markowitz, a graduate student at the University of Chicago, suggested that portfolios could be created that combine different asset classes in a way that would increase return and/or lower risk compared to portfolios of individual asset classes. This approach, now known as modern portfolio theory (MPT), took a total portfolio approach to investing. Incidentally, regulators to this day still look at portfolios as the sum of many disparate parts rather than as a single entity.

Markowitz's big breakthrough was the "efficient frontier," a theoretical combination of risk/return trade-offs that showed how a mix of asset classes might maximize expected returns for any given amount of risk. Of course, quantifying risk tolerance is an exceedingly difficult thing to do. Still, both the approach and the theory behind it became widely accepted. The idea, as expressed through a series of ever-present questionnaires, quantifies the personal tolerance for risk and then aims to maximize returns within that constraint. Portfolio design began a shift from art to science that continues to this day.

Many proponents of evidence-based advice are fans of Nobel Prize winners, since they are the closest one can likely get to being a pure scientist in the fields of finance and economics. Unlike in, say, physics, there are few things that are categorically true in finance, but there are dozens of things that are truer and more reliable than just about anything else. Modern portfolio theory (something that is barely mentioned in course material for advisors) is one of those things, and Markowitz won the Nobel Prize in Economics in 1990.

A well-thought-out investment strategy serves as the foundation for a properly constructed portfolio. Consumers often focus almost exclusively on security selection (including the extent to which investments should be invested actively or passively), while ignoring other associated risks and underlying asset allocations. The offshoot of this advance in thinking is that portfolio development now focuses primarily on reducing risk.

Unfortunately, when advisors end up discussing what consumers and the media think is urgent and appropriate, they often derail their investment process.

Rather than setting their clients straight about what it is they do, they may delude their clients (and themselves) into thinking they have a better sense of where the market is headed, when it will change direction, and which stocks and mutual funds will outperform their peer group.

A good way to illustrate the gravity of the problem is to compare typical investor portfolios to those of pension funds with similar mandates. It has been estimated that approximately two-thirds of all stock holdings in the portfolios of Canadians is stock of Canadian companies. Meanwhile, Canada represents a little over 3% of the world's stock market capitalization. In other words, most Canadians have about twenty times (!) as much money in Canadian stocks than Canadian pension funds do, owing to their worldview of being citizens of Canada as opposed to citizens of the world.

This phenomenon is called home-country bias, and people from every country are afflicted by it. Over-buying in your home market runs contrary to a whole host of well-established economic and portfolio theory evidence. Investors are taking on massive uncompensated risks because they're simply investing "the way their granddaddy did." Knowing what to do and actually doing it are different things. When you're good with a hammer....

Part 1 of the book has argued for a clear differentiation leading to a consistent standard of professionalism—one where there is no confusion between mere sales representatives with licences to sell things and true professionals—often (but not necessarily) with specific accreditations. It has examined the notions of both fairness and respect for competing viewpoints. The time has now come to examine specific bits of evidence to determine for ourselves whether many of the matters discussed here really are mere differences of opinion or something more concrete. Clarity on those matters would greatly assist both consumers and advisors in their decision-making.

In the next section, we'll talk more about the role of the media, specific elements of evidence, and the interplay between how things likely ought to be done and how things are actually being done.

PART 2

SCIENTIFIC TESTING

CHAPTER 5
EVIDENCE-BASED ADVICE

Established professions have a history of operating in a world where the most widely accepted and proven courses of action are the ones that are recommended to clients. In medicine, that involves practitioners keeping up with journals to stay on top of new research. It also involves keeping up with developments of new pharmaceuticals being released after having gone through rigorous clinical trials. It involves surgeons needing to stay abreast of the best new methods, accountants needing to keep up with changes in tax law, and lawyers needing to be mindful of new cases that might put a different spin on precedents.

Looking at hard evidence challenges the easy assumption that some of the most fundamental matters in personal finance are matters of opinion where intelligent people might properly differ. As time goes on, more and more evidence indicates that certain outcomes are likely to yield better results than others. This may prompt you to ask why some advisors continue to do things the old way despite a growing mountain of evidence that supports other ways that are more likely to lead to better outcomes. At the very least, shouldn't their recommended courses of action be the alternatives that are statistically more likely to lead to better outcomes?

The thing that sets professions apart from mere sales-oriented lines of work is their commitment to evidence and process. The "scientific testing" (the "ST" in STANDUP) part is vital. Scientific testing requires that people accept the things that are shown to work and discard the things that don't. It puts emphasis squarely on the things that have demonstrable causal relationships in matters of material importance. Some things might be proven more certainly than others and might need less time to be accepted as a result. For instance, a lot of doctors were smokers when the link between smoking and lung cancer was first verified, but now few doctors smoke cigarettes. Despite sometimes slow changes, the professions nonetheless have a strong commitment to best practices and demonstrated outcomes based on verifiable evidence—and society generally prides itself on the advances that have been made.

One area where people feel some degree of basic satisfaction is regarding scientific progress. Of course, in order for things to get better, we need to actually implement the things we learn. It's all well and good to come up with a better mousetrap, but if no one knows about it, it won't do anyone much good. My opinion is that there could be an opportunity to examine causation here.

A few questions: What if that better mousetrap

were a threat to the status quo? What if a multi-billion-dollar industry had developed surrounding the production and sale of inferior mousetraps? Furthermore, what if there were an army of sales representatives who earned commissions selling these inferior mousetraps?

These are all considerations that are plausible even though they cannot be reliably substantiated. One problem I think everyone would see right away lies with the motives of the inferior mousetrap salespeople—they would never tell anyone about the existence of a better mousetrap!

The Oxford Dictionaries website defines *scientific method* defined as follows:

> A method of procedure that has characterized natural science since the seventeenth century, consisting in systematic observation, measurement, and experiment, and the formulation, testing, and modification of hypotheses.[5]

Perhaps this section of the book will surprise you. As we make our way through it, we'll take a closer look at a few of the more contentious elements of finance to see what the evidence says, what people are doing, and try—as best we can—to identify possible reasons for perceived inconsistencies.

Evidence is important, yet it seems certain circles can be rather selective in accepting what they consider useful information. What if there were evidence that showed past performance is an unreliable metric for product selection, that most people who try to beat the market fail as a direct result of trying, and that the handful of people who succeed are no more than would be expected by random chance and will not persist in their outperformance at any rate? Books such as *The Quest for Alpha* by Larry E. Swedroe and *The Big Investment Lie* by Michael Edesess itemize the research on these matters in greater depth. Let's examine some of these in more detail.

Fund Picking in the 1990s

In the 1990s, something similar was going on. It seemed everyone had a take on how to identify top-performing mutual funds. At the time, it seemed no one could get enough information about what mutual funds were, how they worked, and how to build portfolios using them. Annual fund-ranking books were presumably helpful in allowing consumers to make smart investment decisions. No one publishes books that rank funds anymore. Why not? Furthermore, why did most books disagree on what the best funds actually were? If the research was indeed empirical and predictive, shouldn't they all have identified the same funds? And if the books were so committed to a long-term perspective, why did so many of the recommended funds change from one year to the next—even from the same authors?

Those authors weren't selling timeless and useful information at all; they were simply selling books. And books that need to be updated annually have the handy attribute of built-in obsolescence, meaning they could be tweaked, repackaged, and sold anew twelve months later. From the authors' perspectives, the best thing about these books was their imminent disposability. The second best thing was likely the lack of accountability that the books entailed.

Why would any consumer bother to check the long-term track record of a book from, say, 1996 to see how the recommended funds actually performed by 2016? After all, the thinking goes, whatever was recommended back in 1996 must surely no longer be relevant given all that has happened since. In those days, consumers were always on the lookout for the latest investment idea and could always be counted on to run out and buy the latest version of their favourite rating book the next year. Remember that all the authors told their readers that mutual funds were long-term investments. In reality, many of the recommended funds from a generation ago no longer exist, primarily because their performance was poor.

Perhaps more than anything, these books legitimized stock picking and fund picking as valuable pursuits. These books made no mention of the fact that there was no credible research to support this presumptive value proposition. Specifically, although fund picking had never been done reliably in the past, they implied that it could indeed be done reliably—and people believed them.

In short, the books lent credence to the notion of security selection as an activity that can be reliably used to outperform the markets with no evidence to support it. This lack of reliability is disclosed in prospectuses and advertising campaigns around the world. The books implied that the prospectus disclaimers were worthless when, in fact, it was the other way around.

I took on the challenge of sifting through the most prominent fund-picking books from 1996 (with rankings based on results from June 30, 1995) to see how the ten-year numbers stacked up as of June 30, 2005, and published my findings in *The Globe and Mail*.

The results were stunning. In all four books, the majority of recommended funds lagged their benchmarks over the ten-year period. In fact, a large proportion of the funds weren't even good enough to survive the entire ten-year period. Many studies have shown that survivorship bias causes current performance numbers to look considerably better than they really are. These days, most observers agree that only about 60% of all mutual funds that are launched are around to celebrate their tenth anniversary. Given this attrition rate, it should be obvious that it's much easier to have a respectable class average if you don't have to take a massive dropout rate into account. Regardless, the recommended funds had a collective performance record that could only be described as awful. Perhaps even more disconcerting was that the authors generally used only three years' worth of data to make a pronouncement on a fund's relative merit. In their minds, thirty-six monthly data points were all that was required to make an informed decision regarding performance.

Of course, having most funds lag their benchmarks

after accounting for expenses would make little difference if people could reliably identify the handful that would ultimately outperform. Alas, this can't be done. In fact, by 1998, a ground-breaking research study led by Mark Carhart[6] showed that superior funds could not be reliably identified in advance and do not persist at any rate. I should also add that near the beginning of some of these books, some authors even included passages saying that they believed good managers could be reliably identified. However, no rationale was ever given as to why the authors held this opinion. Then, near the end of these books, they sometimes added astonishing admissions such as "research puts the contribution of security selection—that is, choice of specific investments—at only 2% when discussing performance."[7] In other words, when combining these comments, the translation comes out as something like "we think superior managers can be reliably identified in advance, but we can't prove it, and it is of almost no consequence anyway."

Let's look at this from an advisory perspective. Some commentators have suggested that a primary role for advisors is to assist their clients in avoiding big mistakes. Nonetheless, the advisors who bought into this rationale effectively sold a value proposition that had a questionable basis. Of course, it's tough to position yourself as an expert if you have to admit that your presumptive "value-added service" is tenuous. Note that the same holds true for advisors using individual securities as it does for those using mutual funds. This should be easy enough to follow. If a mutual fund manager can't reliably pick stocks, what makes you think an advisor can do it?

We're left with two possible explanations about the books: The authors either knew their recommendations were dubious or they didn't. If they didn't, then they were guilty of trying to make a few bucks by preying on society's seemingly insatiable quest for disposable information and professing to be able to do something they couldn't. On the other hand, authors wilfully mislead their readers if they know their books are misleading. So which was it? Which is worse? Note that there were three primary stakeholders in this story about misinformation: mutual fund companies, advisors, and retail investors. The writers, fund companies, and advisors, did all right as stakeholders. Retail investors don't fare so well. Since the authors either stated or implied that they believed fund picking could be done reliably, shouldn't they at least have cited a reason for that opinion and then disclaimed the contents of the books as mere opinions?

Why do so many advisors portray themselves as being good fund pickers? Fund picking and stock picking are statistically improbable value propositions in the financial services industry today, but the majority of consumers fail to see it that way.

Benchmarking

Another element of performance is the comparison of mutual funds to one another as opposed to a relevant benchmark, such as the S&P 500 or the TSX. Although the technical definition is more involved, a good way of thinking of benchmarks is to think of something that is widely understood to be a proxy for an asset class. For instance, the TSX is a proxy for large Canadian stocks in total, whereas the S&P 500 is a proxy for large American stocks in total.

Since the vast majority of mutual funds lag their benchmarks in the long run, the industry has chosen to score itself against itself. While published performance tables measure mutual funds against their benchmarks, mutual funds are rated according to their performance relative to other mutual funds rather than in relation to their benchmarks. For instance, you might get a false impression when looking at rankings because the rankings only deal with funds that are still around. There would be 25% of all remaining funds in each performance quartile, yet some funds in the second quartile today would have lagged their benchmark. Remember, benchmarks have no associated costs, but all investment products do. Over a period of two or more decades, fewer than 25% of all (remaining) funds beat their benchmark. One could literally go to a ranking book to find a fund with a ten-year track record that is ranked in the first quartile (top 25% of all funds around for that long). People could buy it thinking they're making a shrewd decision even though the fund may have lagged its benchmark!

By comparing one product to another, the financial services industry creates the impression of a balanced, apples-to-apples comparison. This comparison is fair in a relative sense (i.e., we can see which funds have been better than the others in the past), but that's as far as it goes. In fact, current comparisons might actually prevent you from making a truly informed decision.

The real challenge is in outperforming an appropriate benchmark or lagging that benchmark by the smallest possible amount. That test would be far more meaningful to consumers. It is impossible to buy a benchmark. If you wanted to buy the TSX, you'd be unable to do so. The best anyone can do is buy a product that seeks to track the benchmark in question. All products cost money, so it should stand to reason that a product that tries to match a benchmark is likely to lag by something close to the cost of the product. The most common products used to track a benchmark are index funds and exchange-traded funds (ETFs).

By now, most people have heard of ETFs. They are a sort of hybrid between stocks (because they trade on exchanges) and mutual funds (because they are highly diversified). Not surprisingly, ETFs come in many shapes and sizes and feature many strategies and alternatives. These are summarized briefly later on in the book.

For now, let's concern ourselves with the most basic type of ETF: the type that aims to track a benchmark. We'll discuss other types elsewhere. The oldest and best-known ETFs are concerned only with generating a performance that does not deviate much from a benchmark (known in the business as "minimizing tracking error"). Stated a little differently, if you define risk as "the extent to which my investments deviate from the market as a whole," then traditional benchmark-tracking ETFs are for you. This is just one definition of risk. Many people would define risk as "the potential of losing money," but both approaches have their place.

It might be added that likely the greatest risk of all, market risk (i.e., having your investments drop in value), warrants copious disclosure by the advisor irrespective of the products or strategies chosen. More often than not, an investor will lose money in a falling market and make money in a rising market, and the product decision will make little difference. When choosing between individual securities, mutual funds, ETFs, and other options, an advisor should ideally be able to explain the pros and cons of each and to recommend products and strategies that suit their clients' circumstances.

Similarly, investors should consider their own views regarding risk, reward, and the probability of outperformance when making decisions, and advisors should aim to offer dispassionate advice and guidance to assist them. True professionals offer the most important details of all material facts. The approach should involve professional input based on credible research. Deliberately remaining silent on those same material facts is, to my mind, a form of manipulation.

The Importance of Asset Allocation

One of the most quoted (and misunderstood) papers in the history of finance was one written by three researchers led by Gary Brinson.[8] The research looked into the performance of a multitude of American corporate pension plans and showed that investment policy—the strategic mix of stocks, bonds, and cash—explains over 90% of a portfolio's variance (or risk).

Another interesting bit from the Brinson research showed that pension plans lost an average of 0.66% in returns as a result of market-timing activities. The research further showed that an additional 0.36% was lost as a result of security selection (i.e., stock picking). Would it surprise you to learn that many financial advisors suggest they "add value" with their superior abilities as market timers and/or stock pickers even though such positive outcomes are unlikely?

Previous editions of this book included a chapter entitled "Get an Investment Policy Statement." In the interest of brevity, that chapter is no longer included. Instead, let's look at the four main steps to portfolio design and their implications as indicated by Brinson and his team. These are spelled out as follows at the conclusion of their paper:

1. Deciding on asset classes to be used (which are included, which are expressly not included)

2. Deciding on normal long-term weightings for each of those asset classes

3. Strategically altering the mix in order to try to capture excess returns (market timing)

4. Selecting individual securities in order to try to capture excess returns (stock picking)

The authors showed conclusively that the first two points were critically important, while the second two were of minor consequence. Accordingly, they advised money managers to focus squarely on setting and maintaining a suitable asset mix.

The evidence suggests that investors should focus strategically on investment policy. So why do most advisors focus on the relatively unimportant tactics of market timing and security selection? Even worse, to the extent that market timing and security selection have an impact on performance, the difference seems to do more harm than good, and any beneficial results are outliers, yet many advisors persist in doing things the old way. Again, there are many advisors who, astonishingly, are unaware of the Brinson research even though it is of critical importance and came out a generation ago. I'll leave it to you to draw conclusions.

There's evidence that many people make decisions based on rule-of-thumb shortcuts that often hurt their own self-interest (i.e., performance). There's evidence of factors that consistently explain expected risk and return. Many of these are important enough to warrant their own chapters.

We need to discuss the basic concepts of fact (things based on the best available evidence) and opinion (things that we believe even if we have no hard proof). It seems some people have difficulty in telling the difference.

CHAPTER 6
IS THAT A FACT OR AN OPINION?

Daniel Patrick Moynihan gets the credit for having come up with one of my favourite quotes of all time. He said that while people are entitled to their own opinions, they are not entitled to their own facts. Although many of the perspectives shared in this book are my personal opinions, I would hasten to add that mine are at least considered opinions based on a wide variety of readings and discussions on top of working in the industry for nearly a quarter century. Having an informed opinion basically requires taking the time to carefully consider competing options, viewpoints, and likely outcomes. Obviously, writers and commentators are only human and cannot be absolutely certain about what the future might hold.

Imagine if a doctor had the opinion that smoking cigarettes was not in any way linked to the incidence of lung cancer. The opinions of professional intermediaries are crucial in directing what people do and why they do it. In fields such as finance, it would likely be seen as a stretch to call certain things "facts." However, I believe it is fair to say that many things are proven to be better than others at explaining likely outcomes. While not perfect, I think most people would agree that—all else being equal—professionals should recommend courses of action that generally have the best chance of being successful.

What would you think of a surgeon who recommended a patient proceed with one kind of open-heart surgery over another if you learned that the success rate for the recommended procedure was 80% and that the alternative was successful 95% of the time? Neither option is certain, but I know which one I'd want. I also don't mind if people look at the evidence and choose the less likely option for whatever personal reasons they might have.

It has long been accepted that smoking cigarettes is linked to the increased likelihood of contracting lung cancer. For years, however, that idea was challenged, even by medical professionals. When, exactly, did it make the transition from being plausible to being probable to being verifiably true?

I ask because some people tend to get their backs up when others have the audacity to suggest that what they have believed all their lives just isn't so. Meanwhile, the timing of the general acceptance of evidence is often vitally important. What I believe (my personal opinion) is that it is unprofessional to recommend a course of action that is less likely to yield a positive outcome *without even mentioning that there are alternatives that are more likely to meet your objectives.*

Essentially, every issue known to humanity is either

a matter of fact or a matter of opinion. It is important to note that, while both are well-understood concepts, the expectations surrounding them are quite different. When marketing and providing financial services in a manner that is compliant with regulatory requirements, it is expected that all facts contain a reference where the validity of the concept was first established. In matters of opinion, in contrast, it is expected that the person speaking or writing clearly disclaim the position(s) as being personal opinions and nothing more.

What about matters that aren't entirely clear? What should the standard be? There is obviously no way that regulators can monitor what is said between advisors and their clients behind closed doors. Still, I have encountered individuals in the industry who have expressed their opinions through marketing material without disclaiming them as being their personal opinions. Doing this can easily create a dangerous misconception. Since all personal opinions are to be disclaimed, one can easily conclude that, where there is no disclaimer, the views expressed will be interpreted as a matter of fact. This, of course, further blurs the line between opinion and fact. Advisors and industry commentators are allowed to use both (or either) facts and opinions but are not always clear with their audience about the nature of what they are saying. There are many potential examples of what is considered factual, including the following:

- Research findings determined through the application of the scientific method (preferably sourced from learned journals)

- Empirical data (e.g., market share, average price) provided by reputable sources
- Public opinion research (statistically significant poll results)

Note that certain related items might contain a great deal of professional opinion that is supported by data. This is an instance where everyone can see what is verifiable but where fair-minded individuals might come to differ on what that information really means. In these instances, we start with facts but then slide over to opinions both quickly and seamlessly—sometimes almost imperceptibly.

Let's take a look at the definitions in order to get a clearer understanding about the terms of this discussion. According to the *Canadian Oxford Dictionary*, they are as follows:

Fact: n 1. a thing that is known to have occurred, to exist, or to be true 2. a thing that is believed or claimed to be true 3. a piece of evidence, an item of verified information or events and circumstances 4. truth, reality

Opinion: n 1. a belief or assessment based on grounds short of proof 2. a view held as probable 3. what one thinks about a particular topic or question 4. a formal statement of professional advice (e.g., get a second opinion)

So is it a fact or an opinion when someone suggests that the notion that one can reasonably expect to beat the market is not supported by the weight of evidence? I suppose some would say that the answer to that question could only be gleaned by examining the evidence. Note also that there's some wiggle room in the terminology. For instance, what, exactly, is a "reasonable expectation"?

Let's take a few moments to examine the evidence. How accepting would you expect someone to be in examining a strategy if it had a negative impact on their bottom line? You should always consider the evidence on matters that may or may not be verifiable. You should also be careful to take into account the vested interests of constituencies that might try to persuade you to accept certain viewpoints, as they are less than impartial arbiters of truth. Let's take a look at a few positions that are clearly dominant in the industry today, both in terms of what that position is and what the weight of evidence suggests. The terminology used in these "position" segments is simply my paraphrasing of things that I have heard some advisors say.

Position 1:   "I recommend stock picking strategies (i.e., active management) because my objective is to find active managers who will beat their benchmark."

Evidence: For about a decade now, the people at Standard & Poor's (S&P) have been putting out a semi-annual report called "SPIVA" ("Standard and Poor's Index Versus Active Scorecard"). It is billed as the scorekeeper of the active/passive debate. These reports come out in all major markets, including Canada, the US, Europe, India, Japan, and Australia. "SPIVA" reports cover all one-, three-, and five-year periods, ending on June 30 and December 31. Although the results vary from report to report and region to region depending on market conditions, the index benchmark tends to beat the average performance of active funds quite consistently throughout. Furthermore, the likelihood of benchmark index outperformance consistently increases as the time horizon expands. It is interesting that the reports only go for the most recent five years, but it would be extremely difficult for the folks at S&P to measure performance beyond five years given how many funds fold within five years after they are launched. Stated differently, although the index option generally tends to win, it would likely win resoundingly if the time horizons used were more in keeping with investors' actual time horizons. Most people invest for several decades.

The simple reasoning behind this documented outperformance is outlined in a short paper written by William F. Sharpe in the 1990s.[9] The logic is simple and uses nothing more than basic grade school mathematics. It essentially goes like this:

- The stock market is simply the sum of all active and all passive participants.
- The return for passive participants is the return of the stock market minus costs.

- It follows (given the first point) that the return of the average active participant must also equal the return of the market minus costs.
- Since average active costs exceed average passive costs, the average passive participant must outperform the average active investor.

Note that this is true in all markets (developed and emerging) and in all market conditions (expansion and contraction; inflation and deflation; war and peace), and there are literally no exceptions. In essence, Sharpe isn't saying that the passive horse will win the race because it is faster; he's saying that passive will ultimately win because it has a lighter jockey. Also, in case you're not familiar with the name, please feel free to plug Dr. Sharpe's name into a search engine. He's one of the most respected and influential financial minds alive today, having won the Nobel Prize in Economics in 1990, along with Harry Markowitz. I'd say that this simple and elegant paper is about as close to being a fact as you can get.

Position 2:   "It doesn't matter if the average actively managed product lags its benchmark and/or passive counterpart because I don't recommend average products. I recommend only superior products."

Evidence: To begin, such a statement would not be compliant in the first place since "superior products" is very much subjective. Remember how I noted that people can quibble over individual words? In this instance, the word in question is *average*. There is no evidence that anyone can reliably identify persistent outperformers in advance. There's a reason why every mutual fund prospectus carries a disclaimer to the effect of "past performance may not be repeated and therefore should not be relied upon when making investment decisions." They disclaim this because it's true. Furthermore, this is not the least bit new. Harvard professor Michael C. Jensen first showed how difficult it is to pick winners in advance in an article published nearly fifty years ago.[10]

Almost twenty years ago, Mark Carhart penned what is widely considered to be the first definitive study of the subject to date.[11] He showed that the likelihood of a top quartile fund remaining in the top quartile for subsequent periods was more or less equally distributed. The quartile placement was about the same as throwing darts, with the distributions looking about the same as those generated by random chance. The only performance persistence seems to be on the poor side—lousy funds have a tendency to remain lousy. Perhaps a half dozen similar studies have been published since then, and they all come to essentially the same conclusion: Consistent outperformance cannot be reliably identified in advance.

What is interesting is what was discussed in the previous chapter. In the late 1990s, there were a few annual guidebooks published to "help investors make informed decisions" about the mutual funds they were looking at purchasing. I could not find the slightest reference to either the Jensen research or the Carhart research in any of them. What is particularly disconcerting is that one of those books was authored by an advisor who was governed by regulatory rules about suitable disclosures for marketing material. No suitable disclosures about the research that contravened the fundamental premise were made, and investors were none the wiser.

Position 3:   "Passive products and strategies, by definition, cannot beat their benchmarks. Only actively managed products and strategies have the potential to outperform."

Evidence: This is true but largely beside the point. There's a strong consensus that the primary role of a professional advisor is to get clients retired in the lifestyle they've grown accustomed to. As such, many people feel that beating a benchmark is an inappropriate way of keeping score because the ability to beat a benchmark is largely an unnecessary goal inserted by the active management side of the industry. When I speak with new clients, they almost all tell me that they want me to help them achieve their retirement goals on reasonable terms (i.e., without taking too much risk or sacrificing too much of their current lifestyle). In fact, when I ask my clients open-endedly what I can do for them, virtually none of them say a word about beating a market.

Furthermore, while it is true that an active approach has a greater chance of outperforming a benchmark, it is equally true that it has a greater chance of underperforming that benchmark by a wider margin than the passive alternative. How many proponents of an active approach disclose that the likelihood of significantly lagging a benchmark is greater with active strategies than it is for passive ones?

Let's say you had $100 with two options in front of you: Option 1 gives you a 15% chance of finishing with more than $100; Option 2 gives you no chance of finishing with over $100. In fact, it guarantees that you'll finish with only $99.50. Which do you prefer? If the story ended there, I'm pretty sure many people would choose the first option. But what if those choices were incomplete? What if, in addition to the information above, you were told that Option 1 also gave you a 15% chance of finishing with less than $90 and a 70% chance of finishing with between $90 and $100?

This is still a simplification of the choices, but you can see the problem. Risk and reward are related, and they incorporate the competing concepts of variability regarding both frequency and degree. It's not only about whether you'll do better or worse; it's also about how much better or worse you'll do. Most people are led to think only about frequency, the "odds of success" part of the equation. In so doing, they might not give due consideration to the equally relevant "cost of failure" issue, the degree to which they will be penalized for having tried to outperform. Both are legitimate considerations, but telling only one side of the story is not offering reasonable advice; it is manipulating decision-making by using selective information.

Position 4:   "Even if some active funds don't beat their benchmarks, the costs associated with active management are well worth it. A diversified portfolio containing several actively managed funds that meet your other objectives will compensate for the losers compared to a similar basket of passive products."

Evidence: The empirical results show the exact opposite effect. In 2009, University of Denver professor Allan S. Roth published his book *How a Second Grader Beats Wall Street*. Using thousands of so-called "Monte Carlo" portfolio simulations over differing time periods, he examined the odds of an all-active portfolio beating an all-passive one. In all instances, the odds were reduced as both the number of funds and the time horizon increased. In fact, in comparing competing portfolios of five active funds and five passive funds, the likelihood of the active grouping outperforming was 32% over one year, 18% over five years, 11% over ten years, and 3% over twenty-five years.

The Roth research is far from alone. A recent American study entitled "How Well Have Taxable Investors Been Served in the 1980s and 1990s?" found that the average fund underperformed its benchmark by 1.75% per annum before taxes and by 2.58% on an after-tax basis.[12] It showed that just 22% of the funds beat their benchmark on a pre-tax basis. Importantly, because the issue is not only one of the likelihood of outperformance but also the degree to which an active strategy would add or subtract value, the report showed that the average outperformance was 1.4% but that the average underperformance was 2.6%. However, on an after-tax basis, just 14% of the funds outperformed. The average after-tax outperformance was 1.3%, while the average after-tax underperformance was 3.2%. All told, the risk-adjusted odds against outperformance were pegged at about 17:1.[13] Perhaps most importantly, the odds of outperformance decrease as the time horizon gets lengthier. Note that some investors have time horizons in excess of forty years.

Back to Fact or Opinion

What we have here is a clear disconnect between what evidence suggests and what some practitioners recommend. This disconnect has several potential explanations. We've already touched on how advisors are taught and what their corresponding beliefs tend to be. Traditional business models and value propositions may well be the greatest impediments to moving toward what is best for their clients based on verifiable evidence.

Many advisors have spent their entire careers telling their clients that they "add value" by picking stocks, picking funds, purposefully executing fundamental and technical analysis, getting people into markets as they're about to rise, and getting people out as they're set to plummet. The problem is that they cannot reliably support these claims. In fairness, part of the problem here is that these claims cannot be reliably tested. It is difficult to demonstrate the impact of alternative decisions that, for whatever reason, were not taken.

What is particularly ironic is that many people feel that working with a qualified advisor can significantly enhance many financial dealings. Stock picking, fund picking, and market timing are not among the strategies that are reliable and predictable, but there are many people out there who feel that they offer real benefits nonetheless. These people then make those considerations central to their value proposition. We'll get into those things in Part 3. For now, we'll grapple with how to get advisors to confront the evidence that contradicts many of their own firmly held beliefs.

How does one respectfully demonstrate that a significant percentage of one's peers are fundamentally wrong? To be absolutely clear on this point, no one is saying that these people are not intelligent, diligent, and responsibly client-centred. I'm not disputing that the vast majority of advisors have good intentions. I'm simply saying that the evidence suggests that many of them simply aren't doing what they're setting out to do.

I've frequently told the story of physicians in the 1950s and 1960s doing their rounds and giving away cartons of cigarettes to patients who were stuck in the hospital over the holidays. How do you suppose they felt when the day came where "cigarettes cause cancer" switched over from being a mere possibility—an unproven thesis—to being a simple fact? Those doctors cared about their patients! One day, the Surgeon General pronounced that cigarettes are a leading cause of lung cancer. From that day forward, these physicians were forced to come to terms with their own limitations and professional hubris. Is something similar happening in the financial services industry?

Thinking back to the Sharpe paper, having tens of thousands of stock pickers saying they can beat the market is like having everyone in a class say they can finish a course with an above average mark. No doubt, some people will indeed finish above the class average (benchmark return). The simple point here is that by definition, about half the people in a class will finish with a mark that is below average. Every time someone "adds value" by buying an undervalued stock or selling an overvalued stock, the person on the opposite end of that trade is "subtracting value" by an equal amount. The average is the weighted midpoint of outcomes. To make matters even worse, class averages don't have fees associated with them. Once you account for the fees associated with stock picking, it should come as no surprise that the average participant (net of fees) will actually do a fair bit worse than the benchmark.

At any rate, the issue in all of this is not whether people are allowed to have an opinion. Of course they are allowed. The issue is whether people are manipulating thought processes in order to effectively impose their personal opinions on others who are coming to them for independent advice. The evidence in support of the notion that most stock pickers lag their benchmarks is clearly established. Perhaps a better question would be how society should treat people with opinions that are very far removed from things that are substantiated beyond any reasonable doubt. Is freedom of choice an inalienable right? I've been given many potential explanations about why an advisor might recommend active options nearly exclusively.

The first possible explanation stems from simple habit. Many people start out doing things a certain way and then simply continue doing things that way. There is a view that advisors who have always recommended actively managed products and strategies are merely doing what they have always done and are guilty of failing to change with the times, much like the doctors referenced above.

A second possible explanation is that advisors sincerely believe that, despite the prevailing evidence to the contrary, they can reliably pick securities or products that will outperform their benchmarks and/or peer groups. The view here is that these advisors are earnest in going about their work and legitimately believe that they are doing what is best for their clients. Since there are always examples of products that beat their benchmarks over all time frames, it needs to be acknowledged that this is a plausible explanation. In fact, it largely explains why so many people buy lottery tickets. Just because something is improbable doesn't make it impossible. My concern is regarding the appropriateness of recommending a course of action where a favourable outcome is statistically unlikely. Just because something is possible doesn't make it probable. By extension, if a favourable outcome isn't probable, it is likely not advisable to go down that path without, at the very least, disclosing likely outcomes before proceeding.

Perhaps the most contentious explanation is that some advisors are threatened by the democratizing impact of low-cost, non-embedded products. These are the sorts of people who say things like, "If I recommend passive products, clients won't need me." The irony of this is that people are now caught in the net of recommending products that are likely to be inferior based on the balance of probabilities.

I've been holding a mirror up to my fellow advisors for nearly two decades now. Some appreciate the forced introspection—others not so much. What was once heretical is increasingly viewed as self-evident. I will end this chapter by saying that it is my opinion, and the opinion of a growing number of advisors around the world, that stock picking, fund picking, and market timing are simply not part of the job description of a truly professional advisor.

CHAPTER 7

CAPITAL MARKETS—
EFFICIENCY, FACTORS, AND COST

The previous chapter about evidence might have been a bit premature. As mentioned with the *SPIVA* scorecards, there is a debate that has raged in financial circles for over half a century. That debate is the degree to which capital markets are efficient. In finance, however, the word *efficient* is basically used to describe the extent that markets can quickly and accurately digest and reflect all available information.

On June 23, 2016, the UK voted to exit the European Union. The next morning, when stock markets opened, they were lower all over the world and significantly lower in the UK. The pound sterling was down sharply, oil was down by about $5 a barrel, and gold was up by about 5%. In short, when facts or circumstances change, the markets' ability to reflect those new circumstances is dependent on the level of efficiency. By June 28, markets had stabilized and started moving up again. The correction lasted all of two trading sessions. By the way, why does the industry refer to large drops as corrections but not large gains? Surely, if markets can get things wrong (i.e., need to be corrected), they can do so in both directions.

By now, it should be obvious that the dominant paradigm of the financial services industry is that stock picking is not only valuable but also entirely rational. People hold this view because of the notion that prices are relatively inefficient, meaning that the market is fairly likely to get things wrong and that publicly traded securities are quite often mispriced—sometimes to a large extent—due to the inability of markets to adjust and correct themselves quickly.

To hear traders tell their story, their approach is best because securities are consistently and perpetually mispriced. In short, they believe that markets are fundamentally inefficient. The notion here is to outperform the market through intelligent analysis and by applying a breadth and depth of insight that most individuals could never muster alone.

The fact is that more and better analysis creates greater market efficiency. How can so many people so consistently exploit mispricings only to have those mispricings persist? Any rational money manager would exploit mispricings until there was no more money to be made. At that point, there would be no more mispricings. People who engage in trading as a value proposition simply can't have it both ways.

Most advisors are proponents of active management. This is true no matter what product(s) those advisors are licenced to sell. It is generally true whether or not the advisor in question has a designation. It is generally true whether that advisor works for a large national institution or a small shop. It is generally true whether that advisor is fee-based or commission-based. In short, no matter how you segment the industry, there is a clear preference for active management.

The obvious logical challenge is that if anyone believes they can add value and outperform by trading, then surely they must also recognize that if they are better off as a result of a trade, then the person they traded with is also worse off by an identical amount. All things considered, the two parties to the trade are neither better off nor worse off (although both would have paid transaction charges and one of them might have incurred taxes). The extent to which one party gains as a result of the trade is equal to the extent to which the counterparty loses. Even in a rising market, both sides can make money, but one side will do better at the expense of the other, who will do less well as a result of the trade.

This brings us back to Sharpe's point outlined in the previous chapter. Investing is a zero-sum proposition before costs and a negative-sum proposition after costs. As such, trading does not actually create wealth, but it does redistribute wealth.

The second most obvious challenge to the idea that value is added through trading is this: Why would any mispricing persist? Think of it this way. If a stock were mispriced and trading at $11 when you believed it was absolutely worth $12, how long would you continue to buy that stock? The answer should be that you would buy it right up to the point where the price of the stock hit $12. If you were a portfolio manager looking to make as much money as possible, you'd buy the stock until you had squeezed out every last penny of value. Then what? Well, you'd look for the next mispriced stock and do the same thing. Perhaps you'd sell your overvalued $20 stock that was actually worth $19. You'd sell every share you could for as much as you could, but once the share price dropped to $19, you'd stop.

The logic that the mispricing adherents don't seem to understand is that you can't simultaneously exploit mispricings and still have those mispricings persist after you have done so. Prices are self-correcting. If they are genuinely wrong and people can genuinely make money as a result, then it stands to reason that people will do it until there's no more money to be made. Well, we've got a small army of very smart people using very sophisticated tools and algorithms and techniques to maximize investor returns. Doesn't it seem likely that any mispricings would have been exploited out of existence by now?

Over long time frames, beating the market becomes a finger trap sort of exercise. You've probably seen those little finger traps that you place on two opposing digits; the harder you try to get out, the more difficult it becomes. Money managers are always trying to outwit one another in an attempt to exploit whatever mispricings exist. The problem is that the more they do to exploit mispricings, the less likely it is that those mispricings will exist over time, making the outwitting part increasingly improbable.

As the saying goes, you can't suck and blow at the same time. In other words, even if people could make money reliably through lightning-fast trading, brilliant insights, prescient calls, and insightful analysis, wouldn't all the money associated with those activities have been made by now? How can they quickly and accurately exploit mispricings and still have those mispricings persist after people have exploited them?

Investing is about markets working properly. Another way of saying this is that markets are in equilibrium, where risk and return are fairly reflected and accurately accounted for in prices. In contrast, stock picking is more akin to speculation based on best guesses that employ the premise that markets do not work properly. Making decisions to buy and sell based on often seemingly random events might well be pure speculation masquerading as rational decision-making.

Three Dominant Models of Efficiency

In the early 1960s, Eugene Fama, a graduate student at the University of Chicago, put forward the efficient-market hypothesis (EMH), the idea that prices are pretty much close to being right at all times. Today, Professor Fama is widely revered for having made a lasting impact in his field, and he won the Nobel Prize for Economics in 2013.

The basic concept of market efficiency is the notion that everyone has essentially the same information at the same time and also has the ability to accurately analyze, assess, and act on that information, effectively making it impossible for any individual manager to consistently exploit that information before anyone else does. Put another way, it's nearly impossible for pension fund managers, mutual fund managers, and discretionary brokers to add value through security selection in their well-intentioned work. Ironically, their hyper-competitiveness against one another only ensures greater efficiency of the market.

Economists have a term that explains the added benefit of each additional unit of a product or service: *marginal utility*. If you have fifty analysts, markets might be said to be somewhat efficient. If you have five hundred analysts, markets might be said to be highly efficient. If you have fifty thousand (and the world has far more analysts and researchers than that), you've probably moved to the point where each additional participant actually does more harm than good, since it is doubtful that the final analyst helps with the precision of prices, yet it is certain that the analyst needs to be paid, thereby taking money out of the financial system.

Most people don't suggest capital markets are totally efficient, anyway. It is probably fair to say that there's a consensus among the world's leading academics that markets are sufficiently efficient and that additional attempts to exploit whatever inefficiencies might remain are largely a waste of time and money. Nonetheless, a big part of the industry's mentality is that the market can be beaten and that it therefore makes sense to try to do so, even if some approaches cost more than others.

What He Said

When it comes to discussing potentially contentious topics, some people's opinions are just more credible than others. The more credible people are rooted in evidence, and many have Nobel Prizes in Economics to bolster their opinions. Many of the most reputable people in finance have gone on the record with a simple opinion: You can't reliably beat the market unless you take on more risk than the market. Let's look at some key quotations from esteemed economists and investors.

In his article "The Parable of Money Managers," William F. Sharpe asks, "Why pay people to gamble with your money?"[14] People don't like it when advisors compare active management to gambling, so I won't do that. Instead, I'll simply point out that a Nobel laureate thinks the analogy is a fair one.

There's more. One of the most acclaimed economists of our time is Paul Samuelson, who won the Nobel Prize in Economics in 1970. Here's what he has to say about the subject:

> Ten thousand money managers all look equally good or bad. Each expects to do 3% better than the mob. Each has put together a convincing story. After the fact, hardly 10 out of 10,000 perform in a way that convinces an experienced

student of inductive evidence that a long-term edge over indexing is likely…. It may be the better part of wisdom to forsake searching for needles that are so very small in haystacks that are so very large.[15]

Of course, these are just academics. What do they know about the real world of investing? It's been said that those who suggest something can't be done should stay out of the way of those who are doing it. If it is improbable to beat the market, then why are there conspicuous examples of people who beat it? What about investors such as Peter Lynch and Warren Buffett?

Considered by some to be the greatest stock picker of all time, Lynch had the unique opportunity to select and train his own successor—and the guy he chose couldn't beat the market. So if the "greatest stock picker in history" couldn't pick a good stock picker, what makes people think a less accomplished person can do it? In an interview with *Barron's* magazine in 1990, Lynch was quoted as saying, "Most investors would be better off in an index fund."[16]

Finally, let's see what the Oracle of Omaha has to say. Warren Buffett is perhaps the most revered man in investing today, given his long and laudable track record. Mr. Buffett has recently instructed his heirs to invest their inheritances into a low-cost index fund, but here's what he had to say in a 1996 letter to shareholders:

Most investors, both institutional and individual, will find that the best way to own common stocks is through an index fund that charges minimal fees. Those following this path are sure to beat the net results (after fees and expenses) delivered by the great majority of investment professionals.[17]

Let's assume that "most" (Lynch, Buffett) and "the great majority" (Buffett) of any group is at least 50% + 1. At that rate, over half of all participants should use an indexing strategy. Unfortunately, overconfidence rears its ugly head, and most people think that Lynch and Buffett are referring to someone other than themselves. Well over 50% of the population consider themselves to be above average drivers, too, but we all know that that is statistically impossible.

Note also that Buffet uses the term *investment professionals*. But if advisors are so professional and the evidence in favour of a passive approach is so strong, why do almost all of them recommend an active approach? Do you think it might be possible that overconfidence, competitiveness, corporate culture, an industry history of embedded commissions, and the like might be clouding their ability to give advice?

In his 2005 annual letter to shareholders, Buffett suggested that if Sir Isaac Newton had been a good investor, he would have come up with a fourth law of motion to explain the pitfalls of active management. Here's what he wrote:

Long ago, Sir Isaac Newton gave us three laws of motion, which were the work of genius. Sir Isaac's talents didn't extend to investing: He lost a bundle in the South Sea Bubble [...] If he had not been traumatized by this loss, Sir Isaac might well have gone on to discover the Fourth Law of Motion: *For investors as a whole, returns decrease as motion increases.*[18]

In contemporary terms, that simply means that trading more harms performance. One phrase that some people use is that investment portfolios are like a bar of soap—the more you touch them, the smaller they get.

Evolving Products and Approaches

It might be said that for many years the pre-eminent way of looking at investing was through security selection and market timing. These are the primary tenets of active management as practiced currently. Many of these ideas were first spelled out by the great Benjamin Graham in his books *Security Analysis* and *The Intelligent Investor*, both written before 1950.

More than half a century ago, a man from Princeton named John Bogle created what many now view as the world's first index fund. Instead of doing things the way that Mr. Graham advocated, Mr. Bogle put forward the idea that cost was a major drag on investment performance. Some years (and more than a few slammed doors) later, Bogle founded a mutual fund company called Vanguard. You may have heard of it.

Despite considerable backlash—including allegations that Bogle was "un-American"—Vanguard is now one of the largest money managers on the planet and, at the time of writing this book, is taking in net new assets to the tune of about a billion dollars a day! Mr. Bogle likes to quip that he is less concerned with the efficient-market hypothesis (EMH) than he is with the "cost-matters hypothesis." In essence, he doesn't care about how efficient or inefficient markets are. Rather, his concern is one of simple cost minimization.

In fairness, he has a good point. Many people, me included, are primarily opposed to most active management because of the associated costs. If someone could come up with a competitively priced active product, most—perhaps even all—objections would disappear. By way of example, many people are surprised to learn that about a third of Vanguard's total assets under management are managed actively.

Rather than picking stocks directly or using mutual funds where a manager is trading stocks on behalf of similarly minded investors, traditional index funds aim to replicate the returns of any given benchmark while aiming to minimize both costs and something called tracking error. In essence, many index funds pride themselves on just how accurately they can track their respective benchmarks. Less tracking error means you have a better, more reliable product.

Similarly, a little over a quarter century ago, the

world's first exchange-traded fund (ETF) started trading right here in Canada. In a nutshell, ETFs are a lot like index funds because they aim to track a given benchmark. The difference is mostly one of structure. In contrast to mutual funds, which trade once a day based on the market's closing price, ETFs, as the name implies, trade on stock exchanges throughout the day like a traditional stock.

In the time between the creation of the index fund and the creation of the exchange-traded fund, a third kind of company was founded. In 1981, David G. Booth and Rex Sinquefield, both graduates of the University of Chicago's School of Business (now known as the Booth School of Business) founded Dimensional Fund Advisors (DFA). Dimensional has grown to manage US$414 billion in assets under management as of late April 2016. Booth and Sinquefield had studied under Eugene Fama and were eager to build retail products that would apply his findings.

Occupying the middle ground somewhere between traditional active stock pickers and indexers, the DFA funds added a twist. Some people call this factor-based investing or smart beta. Let's use terminology that is a little less contentious and call it strategic beta. In essence, strategic beta follows certain principles (often referred to as rules) that cause investors to tilt their portfolios in favour of attributes they feel are likely to yield better outcomes.

The folks at DFA effectively straddle a line by aiming for the best of both worlds, using "tilts" toward known attributes that offered historically favourable risk/return trade-offs without incurring the high costs and taxes associated with traditional active strategies. In essence, Eugene Fama and his long-term research collaborator at Dartmouth College, Kenneth French, had shown that risk and reward were related and that it was reasonable to expect above average returns provided that one was willing to take on a reasonable and calculated amount of additional risk to get them.

In essence, strategic beta options offer a middle ground trade-off between traditional active (alpha seeking) products and strategies and traditional passive (beta replicating) products and strategies. This is a relatively contemporary third way of managing money. Given the animosity between the older and more prevailing views, you'd hope the debate and discussion about the relative merits of competing perspectives would be thoughtful and respectful. In fact, the spectrum between paradigms has blurred, but there are still some extremely distinct camps regarding preferences.

While DFA's products are structured as mutual funds, it might be helpful to point out that most traditional passive products and a large percentage of strategic beta products are available using an ETF structure. As of the middle of 2016, there are about 2,300 different ETFs available worldwide. In Canada alone, there are over 470 different ETFs, representing over $100 billion in assets from seventeen different product providers. In fact, the compounded annual growth rate in Canada over three-, five-, and ten-year periods has consistently been over

20%. Most of the rapid adoption of the ETF structure has been in the IIROC (securities) advisory platform.

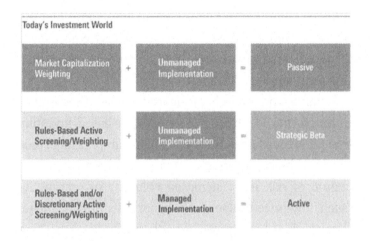

Some people have quipped that the word *smart* in *smart beta* is really just an acronym for "Silly Moniker About Rules-Based Trading." Others have noted with a bit of a chuckle that smart beta implies that it is the opposite of "dumb alpha," which, I suppose, might be another way to describe traditional stock picking. While the terminology has its detractors, the important thing is that people understand what it means when people use it.

Market Equilibrium and the DFA Approach to Investing
New approaches tend to attract attention from the entrenched interests that want to protect pre-existing approaches. Eugene Fama and Kenneth French postulated that higher returns can be plausibly achieved only by taking higher risk. A number of recent studies have

since confirmed this. Since one ought to expect above-market returns only as a result of bearing above-market levels of risk, they came to believe that the term *equilibrium* is more accurate. As an added bonus, the term *market equilibrium* seems to be far less emotionally charged—and far less likely to be manipulated—than the term *market efficiency*.

Fama and French pioneered yet another breakthrough: the identification of a factor-based investing model. According to them (and I am paraphrasing some fairly technical information here), the main characterization of risk is an increased volatility of returns. As such, low-priced value stocks historically provide higher returns than high-priced growth stocks over the long term. Value stocks outperformed growth stocks over most long-term periods. Value stocks tend to be distressed or out of favour, resulting in a higher cost of capital. A company's cost of capital is equal to an investors expected return. For example, it would cost you more to borrow money if you were less creditworthy. Risk and (expected) return are related.

Similarly, they have shown that over the long term, small company stocks have historically provided higher returns than large company stocks over most long-term periods. As one might imagine, small companies usually have a higher cost of capital than large companies, resulting in a higher expected long-term return to investors. Risk presents itself both as increased volatility versus the broad market and as having a greater deviation from broad market returns.

In addition to value and size, other premiums have also been identified over the years, although some of the research is still preliminary. These include momentum, profitability, and, according to some, low volatility. The simple point in this perspective is that one needn't be strictly doctrinaire about the active/passive or inefficient/efficient debate. Simply put, people should do what works in order to make money.

The main characterization of the extra risk explained by how DFA pursues factors is deviation or tracking error from the market. According to DFA, most people don't care much about tracking error and don't use it as a measure of risk. They say that anyone who thinks tracking error is a meaningful measure of risk should use ETFs or index funds that are mandated to minimize tracking error. At any rate, by tilting toward value stocks and small company stocks, the volatility is usually only modestly higher than it is for the broad stock market, but returns have historically been moderately higher.

As far as the people at DFA are concerned, strict index funds are largely flawed. Since index funds are required to buy and sell stocks at the end of the day, they will add or remove stocks (index reconstitution). DFA's research has shown that stock prices are affected even in large liquid markets and that the indexer incurs this extra cost when it happens. In small or illiquid markets, the effect is even more severe.

Rather than rigidly adhere to an index, DFA will delay or accelerate buys and sells to avoid the excessive prices when the index changes. They will buy at a discount when other sellers are anxious to sell large blocks of illiquid shares and then wait through stock momentum to achieve better prices.

DFA also believes the industry could do a far better job of defining proper indexes to be used for benchmarking. Stocks to be included in DFA funds are based on their research into proper index construction and asset class modelling rather than simply following an externally defined index. It might be said that DFA takes an "asset class" approach to investing. The DFA philosophy also includes the following opinions:

- The market return is there for the taking.
- Buying the index will achieve the market return less fees.
- All an investor must do is remain invested.
- If the market return allows an investor to achieve their goals, then take it.
- By intelligently capturing the elements of risk and reward, investors can improve returns.

Perhaps the best way to explain how DFA is different in its approach is to quote founder and co-CEO David Booth: "I recoil when people think that what we do is being passive, because it has nothing to do with being passive. We are trying to beat the market without forecasting in the usual sense."[19]

The Paradigm Bottom Line

It should be noted that there are also disagreements regarding competing passive products and strategies and smart/strategic beta products and strategies. Differing strategic paradigms include strategies such as equal weighting, factor weighting, and fundamental indexing. All involve some amount of sorting by various rules-based tweaks to try to deliver superior returns, either in absolute terms or in risk-adjusted terms. There are also active variations on otherwise passive strategies available—writing covered calls on a pre-set passive basket of stocks, for instance. The main point here is that there are many variations and shades of grey when discussing competing approaches.

It is often dangerous to oversimplify the approaches, so investors need to be careful to truly understand these products before they buy them. Many of them involve some sort of rules-based approach that adds a wrinkle to traditional indexing where the objective is simple benchmark tracking. The larger question revolves around informed consent ensuring that investors know what the value proposition of any product or strategy is and how they might expect that product or strategy to behave over longer periods.

The differences between these competing approaches, while more than a little nuanced, are still modest compared to the differences between them and more traditional active strategies. In summarizing index and equilibrium markets in broad terms, virtually everyone who rejects traditional active management would agree with the following main points:

- Markets work, so traditional stock picking doesn't.
- Diversification is extremely important.
- Cost matters (i.e., you get what you don't pay for).

For the sake of both transparency and accuracy, the underlying assumption for all of this to work efficiently is that stock pickers, innumerable analysts, and the traditional system must continue—otherwise, the "efficiency ecosystem" collapses. My personal view is that we need only about 10% of those players to remain in business in order to maintain a robust mechanism for price discovery.

Since both traditional indexers and strategic beta proponents seem to agree on the vital importance of cost, in Part 3, we'll take a closer look at why current cost is the new past performance in investment products. The importance of cost is both an evidence issue and a disclosure issue. Still, if you have to make a decision about what to buy, I believe you should start by looking at what the products you are considering are likely to cost you over the course of your investing lifetime.

Before we look at cost, however, let's take a look at a couple of other factors that often have a negative impact on your performance: the financial media and our own perverse reactions to how we make decisions.

CHAPTER 8

INVESTMENT PORNOGRAPHY

The challenge for all advisors is to cut through the clutter and to get clients to focus on the things that are both important and within a client's personal control. By the time anyone reads or even hears about financial news, it's too late to act on it. If markets are indeed highly efficient, it means that by the time the information becomes available, larger, faster participants will have already analyzed the implications of the news and acted on it. If there's news that interest rates have gone up unexpectedly, the bond market will reflect that new reality within seconds.

As such, calling your advisor the next morning to act on the "news" is like locking the barn door after the horse has left the stable. The industry has a term to describe the economic and political events that get people interested, even excited, but have virtually no real value: *investment pornography*.

Background Noise

People need to sort out for themselves whether or not it's worth taking action on news items. Developments that are generally unimportant but interesting grab financial headlines on most days. The information is usually nothing more than background noise in the busy hubbub of life for a person seeking financial independence. A large part of the role of an advisor is to act as a filter and to ensure that clients are not unduly swayed by headlines and sound bites. They rarely add up to anything. Investment pornography includes but is not limited to the following:

- fluctuations in currencies
- the prices of oil, gold, and other commodities
- where stock markets closed
- yield curves

Anyone focusing on a time frame of twenty years or longer isn't going to care much about the day-to-day, week-to-week, or month-to-month gyrations of any of these items, but people read about them and people watch the business news daily.

As the saying goes, "In the short run, returns are virtually unknowable, but in the long run, they are virtually inevitable." Advisors with a long-term perspective won't make predictions about what any of the gyrations mean or will lead to because these fluctuations don't genuinely matter in the grand scheme of things. To my mind, professional advisors focus primarily on things that not only matter but are also within their control: asset mix, cost, turnover (taxes), and long-term plans.

STANDUP advisors have a daunting task ahead of

them, yet not for reasons you might intuitively think. If the media goes on and on about sexy tidbits of breaking news, staying focused on mundane long-term goals seems dull in comparison. Long-term, mundane developments are generally not considered newsworthy. As a result, who can blame consumers for thinking the items in the daily news are relatively more important?

It would be inappropriate to imply that all media is focused on the wrong things. There are many excellent journalists and commentators in the media. They have an important job to do. The best articles, pieces of advice, and commentaries are timeless, meaning they are not dependent on current circumstances. "Pay down non-deductible, high-interest consumer debt" is a message that is both important and timeless. "Get in before the price soars" is almost always neither.

Since research supports the notion that trading activity corresponds negatively with performance (meaning the more you trade, the worse you do), the best advice is often to do nothing. Of course, since the business of giving advice has a history of encouraging trading based on the presumptuous notion that trading adds value, you should question anyone who is actively trying to get you to trade a lot. The best investment philosophy is usually to take one's remaining lifetime as one's investing time horizon. That's the time frame that Warren Buffett uses. As mentioned earlier, Buffett has also instructed his heirs to buy low-cost index funds with their inheritance money when he's no longer around.

Speaking from Experience

I've been a regular guest on the television program *Market Call* on Business News Network (BNN) for about seven years now. I enjoy the experience immensely but marvel at how many callers still say that the STANDUP approach is rare among advisors. Since this approach is based on evidence and transparency, it's notable that so few Canadians perceive their advisors as having those qualities. The other thing that I can't get over is that, despite my having consistently said investing is about setting and maintaining a suitable asset mix, minimizing costs and turnover, and rebalancing when things get out of kilter, there are still so many callers who press me for a forecast of some kind. I must admit that when you're live on national television, it is sometimes difficult to find a polite way to tell well-intended questioners that it would be irresponsible to provide a forecast about things that are, by definition, unknowable. That's why people call it news. I also chuckle when people ask me about making a "short-term investment," typically a few months. There is no such thing. By definition, investing is a long-term proposition. Anything short-term is more properly referred to as speculation.

I have no quarrel with people having opinions, including those with opinions different from my own. Some opinions even make for good entertainment. My concern is simply that if we can draw on so much broad, macro-level information, why would anyone want to spend time asking for one person's opinion?

Opinions are like noses—everyone has one. Real value usually lies in providing focus and discipline based on timeless information that must be applied despite an uncertain future.

Unfortunately, as soon as someone is seduced by forecasts, trends, and the like, they become far more likely to do something unfortunate with their money—often repeatedly. Focusing on the wrong things can lead to making bad decisions. The phrase that consultants like to use is "garbage in, garbage out."

Over the years, I've heard more than a few money managers say something like, "This is a good time to use active management." Now, they have their opinion and are certainly entitled to it. How much of an impact does the current market environment have on William F. Sharpe's point that all investing is zero-sum before costs? It would seem to me that all markets are equally good or bad for active management and that the "this is a good time" part is little more than a sales pitch. In reality, all times are equally good or bad—Sharpe's paper referenced in Chapter 6 demonstrates this starkly.

When someone says, "This is a good market for…" it would seem to me that logical follow-up questions might include the following:

- Will you also tell me when it's not a good time for what you just recommended?
- When was the last time when you told people it wasn't so good?
- If you really were looking out for my best interests,

wouldn't you be equally eager to point out when to avoid something bad as when to embrace something good?

The existence of investment pornography complicates the questions surrounding good advice. If good financial advice isn't about understanding trends and making forecasts, then what is it about? If advisors can't add value by getting people to "jump on a hot stock," then what sorts of behaviour can advisors encourage in order to improve the odds of an investor being more successful? We'll look at this question in the next chapter.

If advisors can get their clients to keep their eyes on the things that really matter and can be reliably controlled, they will have likely earned their compensation. Doing so can be difficult when the media, working in concert with an instant gratification culture of consumerism, often distracts people from tried and true principles.

CHAPTER 9

BEHAVIOURAL FINANCE

The phrase "you're only human" is used almost daily in describing the foibles of life, and one of the most interesting aspects of being human is that we sometimes focus on things that are fun while ignoring others that are more purposeful. For consumers and advisors alike, this can manifest itself in some perverse ways.

My view is that professional advisors don't engage in anything other than abstract discussions about the direction or timing of the market or market performance. Everyone who has even implied an ability to make reliable predictions should move immediately to rectify those misconceptions. Consumers and advisors alike should spend most of their time reviewing and adhering to a suitable asset mix and looking for planning opportunities. Beyond that, most of what advisors do might be referred to as "constructive behaviour modification."

Instead of focusing on things that are controllable (cost, asset allocation, tax efficiency), the majority of advisors focus on the most random and uncontrollable element of portfolio design: attempts to enhance performance through security selection and market-timing decisions.

Perhaps it's just more fun to focus on security selection and market-timing decisions. There's not much profit margin available in promoting a steady, suitable, "buy, hold, and rebalance" strategy, even though those things are highly important. On the other hand, there's historically been a whole lot of money to be made in focusing on security selection and market timing.

In Part 4, we'll look at some recent developments regarding what the financial services industry is doing to disclose and manage these conflicts. Until very recently, conflict of interest disclosures were few and far between. Regulators have now made the professional, written disclosure of real and perceived conflicts a necessary precondition of doing business.

I know one successful advisor who has said, "We [advisors] get paid for our opinion." Obviously there are people (such as the advisor's clients) who agree with that, but I disagree. My view is that advisors get paid to explain how things work and assist clients in making responsible, informed decisions based on strategies that take the best evidence into account.

The Big Mistake

Perhaps the main role of a professional advisor is to ensure that clients avoid "The Big Mistake." Of all the advances in the field of personal finance, there may be none more important than certain fairly recent discoveries in behavioural finance. Behavioural finance is the study of how emotional decisions caused by human factors lead to poor investment choices and reduced investment returns. A growing body of research demonstrates how this human side of investment decision-making has a major impact on portfolio outcomes. Despite this, there's no material in any licencing textbook to teach advisors how to stay the course and deal with problems caused by their clients' emotions.

The research that these thought leaders conduct is about as compelling and important as any. They have shown that large proportions of society are susceptible to decision-making quirks that are often self-destructive. This evidence presents an obvious challenge for advisors. On one hand, changing behaviour can be emotionally difficult, so people instinctively resist it. On the other, not changing can lead to considerable losses. When people are confused and anxious, they tend to do irrational things such as sell low and buy high, even as they profess to be sensible long-term investors.

On the surface, many consumers have sufficient knowledge of capital markets to make adequate financial decisions. Despite this, the data on fund flows shows massive net redemptions when mutual fund values are dropping and massive net sales when markets are on fire. If the phrase "buy low, sell high" is such a trite little truism that anyone can understand, why do so many people do just the opposite?

Similarly, if the principle of diversification is so basic that it is seen as a motherhood issue that everyone understands and agrees with, why were so many portfolios wildly overweight in technology when the bubble burst at the turn of the millennium? There is considerable evidence of home-country bias everywhere on the planet. Why do citizens of every nation on earth invest disproportionately in domestic stock markets? If they're all seeking the best possible risk-adjusted return, it should be obvious that they can't all be right in how they're investing. It seems the quest for performance can easily take a back seat to convenience and familiarity.

If left to their own devices, consumers will frequently make emotional decisions during market swings and manias, even if they later acknowledge in hindsight that they were not making logical decisions at the time. As such, an advisor might be able to apply the teachings of behavioural finance to help clients maintain a better sense of perspective. That, in turn, should lead to better decision-making.

Qualified advisors can be useful in offering reasonable counsel that would prevent self-destructive tendencies. STANDUP advisors understand this intuitively. Despite this, advisors receive no formal training in the field of behavioural finance before they start in the business. Licencing exam course material does nothing to explain behavioural concepts such as anchoring (relying too heavily on the first piece of information offered) or loss aversion (preferring to avoid losses over acquiring equivalent gains), even though these and other emotional and intellectual blind spots go a long way in explaining investment experience.

Advisors should understand that they need to offer advice from the client's perspective and that the client is going to feel overwhelmed by some of the complexity and uncertainty of capital markets. University courses leading to an advanced degree in financial planning, therefore, also need to add an entire body of work to their course material dealing with tangible case study approaches on how to assist clients in staying the course and avoiding "The Big Mistake." Imagine the good that qualified advisors could do if educators actually taught them how to apply solutions to these problems.

Behavioural Evidence

Daniel Kahneman is one of the most influential social scientists of our time, but relatively few people have heard of him. In 2002, Kahneman was awarded the Nobel Prize in Economics together with Vernon Smith. What's interesting is that Kahneman is a psychologist. He and his long-time collaborator, Amos Tversky, offered copious evidence that the most basic assumptions of modern economics do not actually hold when tested with real people. Their groundbreaking research in the field of decision-making has precipitated a sea change in finance.

Kahneman and Tversky's research is about as compelling and important as any research out there. They have repeatedly shown that large proportions of society are susceptible to decision-making quirks that are often self-destructive. They specifically showed that humans are frequently less than rational in making decisions within the context of uncertain outcomes and that people have difficulty in processing probabilities and maintaining a consistent stance depending on how propositions are framed.

The Kahneman and Tversky research is particularly interesting when combined with what won the Nobel Prize in Economics the previous year. In 2001, the Nobel went to Joseph Stiglitz and others for their work on markets with asymmetric information (where people on one side of a transaction have better information than people on the other side). This is an obvious problem with financial advice, since advisors tend to know more than clients and there is usually some degree of reliance involved. As we will see in Part 3, there are "agency issues" when an advisor is called upon to offer guidance, but that guidance may be biased.

While some experts believe there are investors out there who can exploit human foibles for personal gain, Dr. Kahneman doesn't think it can be done reliably. Based on his own findings, he is of the view that markets are highly efficient. He says:

> People see skill in performance where there is no skill.... People are overly impressed by the performance of money managers, who sell what they've been doing for the past few years. It is difficult to realize that you would get very similar patterns if there were no skill at all in picking stocks or running funds.[20]

He goes on to say that:

> [...] the idea that any single individual without

extra information or extra market power can beat the market is extraordinarily unlikely. Yet the market is full of people who think they can do it and full of people who believe them. This is one of the great mysteries of finance: Why do people believe they can do the impossible? And why do other people believe them?[21]

Many advisors would be well advised to consider the three possible ways of processing information:

- You could know something and know that you know it.
- You could not know something and know that you don't know it.
- You could not know something and be totally unaware of your own ignorance.

This last situation is usually the most dangerous. I suspect there are advisors who don't recommend certain products and strategies because they are simply unaware of the evidence in support of them. My view is that these advisors are doing a disservice to their clients.

In contrast, advisors can be useful in offering reasonable counsel that comes from a perspective that should mitigate potentially self-destructive tendencies. Again, advisors receive no formal training in the field of behavioural finance before they start in the business. This is an area where case studies could likely be used to help advisors transition from textbooks to real world scenarios.

Ironically, Kahneman and Tversky are also two of the biggest allies that stock pickers and fund pickers have. People engaged in the business of security selection argue that if people make repeated mistakes regarding risk and reward, then clearly capital markets must not be altogether efficient. The behavioural finance research deals with individual decisions made by particular investors, whereas the market is actually the sum total of all investors (private and institutional, large and small) who react to information as it becomes available. Therefore, even though individual investors might make inappropriate investment decisions, the market as a whole might not. Errors can be high or low, early or late. Since they are more likely than not to cancel each other out, the current price of any security at any point in time is largely fair, making it nearly impossible to exploit a mispricing for profit.

A STANDUP advisor might be able to apply the teachings of behavioural finance to help clients maintain a better sense of perspective. That, in turn, should lead to better decision-making. There's an old saying in poker: If you look around the table and can't figure out who the patsy is, then chances are that you're the patsy.

Daniel Kahneman's critically acclaimed international bestseller *Thinking Fast and Slow* was originally published in 2011. It makes the distinction between two basic, oversimplified models of decision-making—something he calls System 1 and System 2:

- System 1 is nearly spontaneous and often wrong.
- System 2 is more methodical but chronically lazy.

Kahneman is interested in how people actually make decisions—in stark contrast to the prevailing thinking of almost all economic modelling. Notably, he challenges the basic universal premise that people are sensible, consistent, rational, self-interested, and utility-maximizing. He showed that people often make decisions that are less than that. It seems we humans give ourselves more credit than we deserve.

In terms of explaining why most advisors prefer traditional active management, it should be obvious that the decision of many advisors to favour the active camp may be nothing more and nothing less than a simple decision to be persuaded by a narrative that, on the surface, seems plausible and to leave it at that without investigating further. In other words, perhaps many advisors who default to system 1 (a spontaneous reaction) do so because they simply dislike system 2 (being chronically lazy). It doesn't hurt the sales process if most would-be customers share this seemingly reasonable but unsubstantiated viewpoint.

A large percentage of advisors in the business today have never even heard of Kahneman, and most began giving advice before his groundbreaking work was recognized at any rate. These advisors likely advise the way they do simply because that's the way they've always done it. As with the physicians who once thought cigarettes were, at worst, harmless, this might be a simple case of ignorance. Peer pressure and groupthink might also play a role.

One example in the book is the so-called "fourfold pattern," where Kahneman and Tversky showed how people are risk-averse when there's a high probability of a gain and a low probability of a substantial loss but are risk-seeking when there's a low probability of a substantial gain and a high probability of a substantial loss.

Kahneman and Tversky showed that most people are inconsistent in their decision-making and that cognitive biases abound. The outcomes associated with competing choices are often uncertain. People are allowed a reasonable degree of latitude to interpret things (data, trends, research reports, etc.) in whatever manner they see fit and to make recommendations accordingly. The problem is that we all have biases.

What about trade-offs? If there are two competing courses of action and neither is certain to lead to a better outcome, but one is far more likely than the other to lead to a better outcome, can someone reputably advocate for the less likely option without even mentioning the option that is more likely?

This goes straight to the heart of decision-making because it goes straight to the heart of advice-giving, which, in turn, involves the long-accepted principle of informed consent. How does one provide responsible counsel in a world where some outcomes may be more probable than others but, at any rate, no course of action is unambiguously superior in all instances? How much detail is required? How thoroughly does the client need to understand the options before taking action?

Returning to how advisors are prepared in the first place, I believe the system effectively sees to it that advisors are precluded from pointing out deficiencies and questionable assumptions on how to give advice once they launch their careers. Conversely, when someone from outside the industry tries to suggest reforms, that person is often shunted aside as a mere journalist or academic who has no idea what it's like in the real world because they don't have to deal with retail clients every day. In essence, when trying to incorporate new approaches, the people inside the industry are silenced and the people outside the industry are marginalized and dismissed. Real progress proceeds at a glacial pace.

Some people might say that the ideas explained by behavioural finance are too new and therefore not particularly reputable. I find that amusing. The idea of risk-averse decision-makers preferring options that maximize utility (as opposed to economic value) was first put forward by Swiss scientist Daniel Bernoulli in the 1770s. The concepts are hardly new. Meanwhile, the nearly universal acceptance of Kahneman and Tversky's work—itself more than decades old—speaks to how reputable it is.

Other highly respected behavioural economists underscore both the importance and the broad acceptance of this field. People such as Richard Thaler at the University of Chicago, Dan Ariely at Duke University, and Dilip Soman at the University of

Toronto are all renowned thought leaders in the field. They would say to traditional economists that it's all fine and well to theorize what people ought to do and then note that the rubber only hits the road when applying the scientific method to what people actually do.

Accordingly, there are many biases that we all need to be aware of. The idea of decision-making (sometimes called "prospect theory") as being clear, consistent, and rational has been shown to be anything but for nearly everyone. It seems as though people engage in decision-making shortcuts where Kahneman's spontaneous System 1 usually holds sway over the more thoughtful, purposeful System 2. There are perhaps dozens of cognitive errors that people (including unwitting advisors) make routinely. Obviously, the first step toward reducing these errors is to learn about them so that we can be mindful of them. Let's take a quick moment to go over a few of the most prominent errors people make:

Cognitive Error	Example
Overconfidence	People just seem to think they're better investors than they really are. This is especially true of men. I once saw a picture of a billboard that read, "Every year, thousands of men will die due to stubbornness." Underneath it, someone (a man, no doubt) wrote, "No we won't." Lest you think advisors are alone in the professions regarding overconfidence, you might be surprised—or vexed, depending on your perspective—that scientists, lawyers, engineers, and doctors also suffer from it.
Hindsight bias	This is where people insist that they "saw it coming all along" when, in fact, they didn't. Things don't always turn out the way we expect them to at the outset.
Attribution bias	This is where people take credit when things happen the way they expected them to. Of course, if things don't go the way they expected, they put it down to chance: "Heads, I'm smart; tails, I'm just unlucky."
Confirmation bias	This is where people generally

| | look for information that supports their pre-existing viewpoint (the utility of stock picking, perhaps) without spending a similar amount of time and effort in attempting to uncover evidence that invalidates or challenges their position. |
| Status quo bias | This is where people just keep on doing what they've always done due to simple inertia. |

There's also tunnelling, herding, mental accounting, loss aversion, the endowment effect, and representativeness—to name only the more prominent cognitive biases. The list goes on. An excellent resource for those who want to learn more about how behavioural finance forced its way into the mainstream is Richard Thaler's *Misbehaving*, first published in 2015.

Thaler uses dozens of examples, many of them uproariously humorous, to show how the behaviourists have challenged traditional economists with anomalies that the traditionalists cannot explain. There is a seemingly endless supply of examples of human behaviour that simply doesn't square with the traditional economist paradigm of rational choice. Note that one potential pitfall is choice overload. Realistically, there are only so many options that a mind can focus on at once. People might wonder how much detail is actually required.

Much of Thaler's findings also have to do with the

concept of framing, which is simply a matter of decision-making based primarily on how the options were presented to you in the first place. For instance, it has been shown that if you put healthy options near the front of the buffet counter in a cafeteria, people are more likely to choose them, but if you put the junk food near the front, people will choose those. Note that all options are available in both instances. The only difference is where and when you actually see them and are forced to decide on what to put on your tray as you remain in line heading to the checkout.

Before writing *Misbehaving*, Thaler wrote another bestseller entitled *Nudge*, co-authored with Cass Sunstein of Harvard in 2008. Their big idea was "choice architecture," where decision-making could be guided toward desired outcomes via little "nudges" like the one in the cafeteria example. However, the glorious term that Thaler and Sunstein coined was *libertarian paternalism*, which is basically the idea of giving people a wide menu of choices but setting up the options in such a way as to encourage desired outcomes. Retail clients often choose from a wide menu of options, but their advisor might present the menu in a way that encourages choices that favour the advisor's preferences. These can be choices regarding products, value propositions, business models, and the like. Again, if you're good with a hammer….

In my view, the industry still has serious issues and is in need of urgent repair. Meaningful options have been slow to appear, however. Many advisors continue to recommend more expensive products and strategies instead of less expensive ones. Many use transaction business models instead of fee-based ones. There are those who are paid using convoluted and opaque compensation structures when simpler, transparent alternatives exist. The only changes that have occurred thus far have been made one by one with advisors transitioning from the old paradigms to the new ones. The good news is that many advisors have shifted their practices to be more transparent, cost-sensitive, and client-centric.

Public policy "nudges" have been incorporated into the legislative framework of virtually all developed nations around the world. In other words, the ideas listed above are not just a bunch of curious quirks and neat ideas; they collectively represent something that is absolutely being implemented already. Perhaps you've noticed the nudges, perhaps not. Meeting reminders, GPS systems, update notifications on computers, alarm clocks, and calorie-counting apps all count as different forms of nudges. The health warnings on cigarette packages are nudges, too. All over, people are making smarter, better choices without ever being told what to do.

The New Keynesians

The emerging role of the professional advisor is both interesting and unique. On one hand, we're talking about people who know minute details about financial concepts that most people never think of. On the other hand, advisors have to stay tuned to their clients' deepest emotions if they ever hope to gain the necessary trust to get them to act in ways contrary to their potentially dangerous natural instincts.

In short, a good advisor can be a valuable resource in understanding many concepts. The profile of a new type of advisor is already taking shape. Many believe that being a trusted advisor in the future will likely go well beyond simply managing money. Advisors will also have an important role to play in educating their clients about themselves. The word *educate* comes from the Latin *educere*, which literally means "to draw out." Good advisors will ultimately need to draw out their clients to allow them to better understand—and help—themselves. Nudges would be helpful. One example of this might be a simple e-mail reminding clients of the need to maintain a long-term perspective when markets are experiencing short-term turmoil.

Let's use the ideas of another well-known economist to illustrate the coming together of both conventional economics and behavioural economics when explaining the role of a professional advisor. John Maynard Keynes was an extremely influential economist who felt that the primary role of governments was to smooth out the business cycle—to have highs that were less high and lows that were less low—while still growing the economy. He believed that governments should spend more money (perhaps incurring a deficit) to stimulate the economy when things were slow and then spend less (or tax more) when times were good to make up for any previously incurred shortfalls.

Keynesian economics is likely more universal than you might think. Instead of looking at the financial stability of a nation, why not compare this with an individual household? Advisors play a role with their clients that can be likened to what governments try to do when implementing Keynes' ideas: get them to do things they might not otherwise be inclined to do.

Human nature being what it is, clients are often inclined to buy when things are going up and to sell in a panic when the markets are heading down. The role of a good Keynesian public policy administrator is to constructively temper the highs and lows of the business cycle for the greater good of the public. The parallel role of a good advisor is to temper the highs and lows of client emotions. There's a distinct need to help people resist the temptation to buy just because the investment has been going up or to sell just because it has been going down. It is intellectually simple for nearly everyone to understand but not all that easy for many people to do.

Trade Less to Save Tax

Despite this situation, good advisors can be useful in helping their clients deal with some of the insights of behavioural finance. Irrational trading tendencies can have another negative consequence: tax liabilities. A recent study showed that taxes eat up as much as one-sixth of the average mutual fund return, which is only 9% to begin with. Since most mutual funds in Canada are held outside registered plans, this is a significant concern. Amin Mawani, Moshe Milevsky, and Kamphol Panyagometh of the Schulich School of Business at York University in Toronto have researched the effects of taxation on mutual fund portfolios. In a recent study published in the *Canadian Tax Journal*, they conclude that "taxes exceed management fees and brokerage commissions in their ability to erode long-term investment returns."[22] It is widely believed that a responsible advisor can help consumers resist making questionable trades. In the United States, legislation now compels mutual funds to disclose after-tax returns. The Schulich research turned up some interesting results, including the fact that when funds are ranked for their after-tax returns, the order generally differs from rankings of pure fund performance. On average, funds moved up or down twenty-eight spots in the rankings compared to their peers as a result of their tax efficiency (or lack thereof). Buffett's joke in Chapter 7 about Newton's potential Fourth Law would certainly change the way some people invest—if only they were aware of the evidence!

Biases don't only exist in terms of what one buys; they also exist in terms of when one sells. Nearly every major study on the subject has shown that portfolio turnover correlates negatively to performance. The more you trade, the worse you do on average. Every trade involves costs, including transaction costs, bid/ask spreads, and possible tax liabilities. Most people trade too much. This often happens because people believe they can discern trends when random events cause prices to display trendlike attributes. Experts consider this to be clear evidence of overconfidence.

It's one of the great ironies about wealth management. Many people assume that in order to stay on top of your finances, you need to monitor them constantly and to make swift, sure, and informed decisions when circumstances change. Few things could be further from the truth. As it turns out, many of the most successful investors are strategic thinkers who are prepared to wait years for things to pan out.

This is another area where advisors can add value. They can act to encourage their clients to trade less by insisting that perceived trends are actually nothing more than random outcomes and not the sorts of things that one should consider useful information.

Watch Your Behaviour

Until perhaps thirty years ago, investment management and advisory were strongly dominated by transactional advisors (meaning advisors got paid only when clients completed trades) or commission-based advisors (meaning advisors got paid only when clients bought something). Today, there are two clear camps. One camp sees turnover at an all-time high level, whether using individual securities or mutual funds where the manager is trading the underlying securities at an unprecedented rate. The other sees people moving predominantly to an approach that buys, holds, and rebalances from time to time using products that are mostly cheap, pure, broadly diversified, and tax-efficient.

Research done at the University of Michigan and published in 2005[23] showed that purchase decisions made by mutual fund investors are influenced by salient, attention-grabbing information and that investors are typically more sensitive to in-your-face fees such as front-end loads and commissions than they are to operating expenses. As a result, people are more likely to buy funds based on performance, marketing, or advertising. The research showed a consistent negative relationship between flows and front-end load fees. In contrast, they found no relation between operating expenses and new money flowing into the funds. It seems that by getting people to focus on top-of-mind considerations such as returns, you can get them to overlook mundane things such costs that are actually quite important.

The research showed that marketing and advertising (things that are generally embedded in fund operating expenses) accounted for this. The findings lend credence to the notion that mutual funds are sold, not bought, and that behavioural factors normally associated with poor consumer decision-making (such as being fairly oblivious to price) caused people to make some perverse decisions. We'll talk more about purchase decisions in Part 4. There's some important new Canadian research on the subject that's just been completed.

The financial services industry grew out of a sales culture that made money by engaging in trading activity. Unfortunately, there was no way for consumers to determine whether the advice to make a trade was genuinely in their best interests. Over time, individual securities were replaced by mutual funds as the investment vehicles of choice for most consumers. Recently, ETFs have been gaining market share at the expense of mutual funds. No matter what it is you trade, however, it seems you will likely be better off if you do less trading.

Only the most recent generations of MBA graduates have been taking mandatory courses in ethics. Similarly, new university graduates with a degree conferring the right to practice as professional and holistic financial advisors will need to address the very real gap in the education system as it presently stands. Newly minted advisors may have to write some essays, role-play with their classmates, and participate in interactive learning in diagnosing both the financial and the emotional distresses facing prospective clients. An entire generation of advisors has never been taught the importance of behaviour in offering advice. New advisors may continue down the same path as those before them because no one ever showed them how to focus on these important things. Ironically, they missed out on them because they were too focused on the things they presumed to be important but were, in fact, unimportant. Providing focus and discipline is crucial—so is leading by example.

In my view, no matter what products advisors are selling and what services advisors are providing, it should be clear that many traditional advisors have not kept up with evolving approaches and long-established evidence, which is what any reputable professional should do as a simple matter of course. Professional advisors should do the following:

- Think like professionals
- Focus on problem solving
- Focus on client goals
- Show considerable concern for cost
- Understand client behaviour

Since we now know that everyone has some degree of bias in their thinking, what steps could we take to confront this problem? Having looked at the problems with incorporating evidence, we can now turn to the problems associated specifically with giving advice. The desired outcome is to overcome these problems wherever possible. Irrespective of what an advisor knows, the rubber hits the road when they sit down to give advice to their client...and have a positive impact on what that client does with their money.

PART 3

NECESSARY DISCLOSURE

CHAPTER 10
COST MATTERS

Where to put a chapter on product cost? On one hand, the evidence is clear that cost is likely the most reliable determinant of long-term performance. On the other, what good is evidence if no one feels compelled to disclose it? Ultimately, I came to the conclusion that the recognition of the critical importance of cost was primarily a disclosure issue.

The importance of cost is something that some advisors seem to be unaware of—or at least unconcerned about. You know how mutual funds all carry disclaimers about past performance not being a reliable indicator of future performance? It seems no one pays much attention. My experience in speaking with hundreds of advisors who recommend mutual funds to their clients is that their primary consideration regarding recommendations is past performance. However, they pay little attention to product cost. Meanwhile, the evidence is overwhelming that product cost is the more reliable performance predictor. The reason for this is simple: Costs tend to persist, while performance does not. In other words, products that are cheap today are likely to be cheap tomorrow. Meanwhile, products that perform really well today (or this quarter, or this year, or…) are likely to revert to the mean with poor performance down the road.

In terms of professionalism, there's an obvious lesson here regarding not only what advisors generally do but also why they do it. Most people would agree that a true professional should advise a client to pursue a course of action that offers the best probability of a successful outcome, all things considered. The reality is that there are advisors who still think and act like salespeople. Since some clients think past performance is important, it might be that advisors act as though that's the case. Clients also seem to think that product costs are unimportant—so, again, advisors might act as though that's the case. Notwithstanding what clients think, some advisors might actually think past performance is more important than cost. Is that because they are unaware of the evidence or because they reject it?

Anyone can look at a table of competing products and see for themselves which is the cheapest, just as they can look to see which products performed best. So why would anyone pay for either service? The sense that most people have is that advisors like to tell good stories rather than look for hard evidence. It's just so much more interesting to talk about how you've met the manager and how you understand and appreciate his unique process. Never mind that simply sorting for cost probably works better.

The problem is that the arithmetic of money management is irrefutable: *You get what you don't pay for.* It may well be that financial products are the only products in the world where quality correlates negatively with price. With virtually everything else you name— wine, art, clothing, automobiles, household appliances—the best products generally cost more. That's not necessarily so with investment products. Since product cost eats away at your total return, the best investment products—on average, because there are always going to be exceptions—are the cheapest.

For decades, a Chicago-based consulting company called Morningstar has regularly released star ratings for mutual funds around the world. The ratings (better past performances means more stars) have been shown to be a major driver of net new mutual fund sales. Over time, it became perhaps the best way to determine which funds would be bestsellers. The funds that got only one star usually ended up seeing net redemptions, those with two and three stars got very modest sales, and those with four and five stars saw disproportionately large net new sales flow into them. There can be no doubt that for over a generation, money followed performance and the correlation was obvious to everyone.

Imagine the surprise the industry felt a few years ago when Morningstar acknowledged that if you simply chose one of the cheapest funds in any given asset class, you were likely to do better than if you picked one of the five-star funds. For over a generation, people were measuring the wrong thing. They've recently updated their research, and the most recent version of their study says:

> Costs really are good predictors of success. We've done this over many years and many fund types, and expense ratios consistently show predictive power.[24]

To this day, low cost is still likely the best predictor of future returns, and strong past performance (combined with the existence of trailing commissions) is still easily the best predictor of current sales. Old habits die hard. Having gotten into the habit of measuring and recommending investments based on past performance, there are advisors who continue to do so, even when there are more accurate yardsticks available.

I've asked the folks at Vanguard to put together a spreadsheet to help readers understand the full impact of cost differentials on their long-term performance. The base case scenario looks at a portfolio generating a 6% total return (most experts would agree that this is a reasonable long-term expectation for a balanced portfolio of diversified benchmarks).

Note that in this 6% scenario, there is no product cost (which is actually impossible, because you cannot buy a benchmark for free) and no advice cost. To get a better idea of the sensitivity regarding the various cost leakages, let's make some simple assumptions about what these costs might be. I'll use a range to reflect realistic possibilities, but then I'll recommend a single number within that range so that you can mix and match expenses for yourself. Here are the assumptions:

Product	Cost
Individual stocks and bonds	0%
Exchange-traded funds	0.1% to 0.6% (assume 0.5%)
F-class mutual funds	0.9% to 1.8% (assume 1.5%)

Type of Advice	Cost
Do-it-yourself (discount brokerage)	highly variable (assume 0%)
Robo-advisor (algorithm-based)	0.3% to 0.6% (assume 0.5%)
Human advisor	0.9% to 1.4% (assume 1.0%)

There are zero added value assumptions for active managers, which is consistent with the thesis that active management, on average, provides no predicted added value to returns. For us to understand the cost of building blocks for both products (i.e., portfolio "parts") and advice (i.e., portfolio "labour"), it might be best to focus on the cost differential. For instance, the average ETF might cost less than 0.5%, and the average F-class mutual fund might cost less than 1.5%, but I think it's fair to say that, at any rate, the cost differential is likely to be around 1%. Again, this is a simplification. Actual dollar amounts, percentage amounts, and final results will vary. You are also free to mix and match products within accounts.

Now that we have the tools to mix and match products and services, we can now look at the performance drag associated with each of the options. Of the nine possible combinations, the only ones that don't really exist right now are using a robo-advisor to buy something other than ETFs and having a DIY investor buy F-class funds. Unless you insist on getting face-to-face advice, the other combinations are available virtually anywhere in the country. Buying individual securities with no associated advice is certainly the cheapest option, but it involves taking certain stock-specific risks that could be diversified away with other options. Remember that the total cost is the sum of the product cost and the advice cost.

	ETFs	F-class mutual funds	Individual securities
Robo-advisor	1.0% (0.5% + 0.5%)	N/A	N/A
Human advisor	1.5% (0.5% + 1.0%)	2.5% (1.5% + 1.0%)	1% (0% + 1%)
DIY	0.50%	N/A	0% + trading costs

To repeat, the total cost is the sum of the two constituent costs: parts (product costs of the ETFs, mutual funds, or securities) and labour (products associated with advice). Buying ETFs through a robo-advisor might cost about 1.0% (0.5% + 0.5%) in total; buying those same ETFs through a human advisor might cost 1.5% (0.5% + 1.0%), but buying F-class mutual funds through a human might cost 2.5% (1.5% + 1.0%).

The concern that many people express is that most Canadians want and absolutely need financial advice. Furthermore, it is questionable whether many of those same Canadians can afford the risks associated with buying individual securities, since they absolutely should be diversified and it is likely difficult to build a truly diversified stock portfolio if you don't have a seven-digit account.

To date, only a handful of Canadians (typically millennials, but also some small investors) have engaged the services of robo-advisors. That may change, but for now, the percentage of people using robo-advisors still rounds to zero. Similarly, most people who feel able enough to manage money themselves will likely use whatever building blocks they feel are most appropriate.

The real test, therefore, is in comparing people who want and need human advice. Only the wealthy are likely using individual securities as portfolio building blocks. The rest of us will have to choose between mutual funds and ETFs when working with an advisor. What does the chart below tell us?[25]

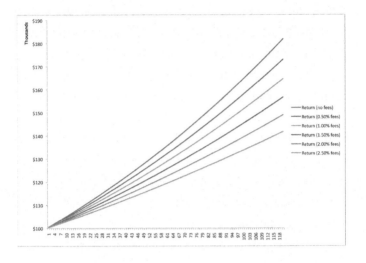

We're using a simple $100,000 starting point because most people reading this will accumulate that amount at some point in their lifetime. We're also using it because it's a simple number to use. If you want to test assumptions using your current circumstances but have only $50,000 to invest, then simply cut the numbers in half. If you have $200,000 invest now, simply double them.

We know that this model is basic, because most people will actually add to or subtract from their portfolio over time. Furthermore, remember that most people's timelines are longer than they might think. We're all living longer these days. It is entirely reasonable to expect someone who is forty years old to have accumulated $100,000 and to live for another forty years after that point.

Accordingly, if this fictional forty-year old were to

invest $100,000 now and earn 6% minus a 1.5% cost leakage (human advice with ETFs), he'd end up with $602,932 at age eighty. If his twin sister were to invest $100,000 over the same time frame using mutual funds, she'd end up with only $404,695—a difference of just under $200,000. That is likely the biggest aha moment most Canadians still haven't had. Most people significantly underestimate the effect a 1.0% difference in costs would have on their terminal wealth. Virtually everyone reading this book could add a six-digit amount to their ultimate net worth simply by cutting their costs. Of course, charts are nice, but we're told a picture is worth a thousand words. So here's a graphic illustration of the point:[26]

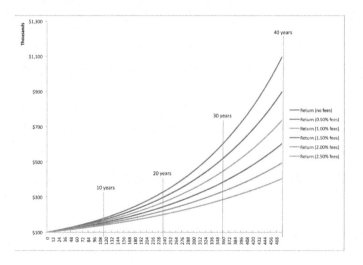

There's nothing quite like seeing how the ongoing, silent impact of costs can erode your wealth. As mentioned previously, many people in the financial services industry change the subject when I talk about cost. The divergence is in the distinction between cost and value, because every time I start about cost, they counter with arguments about value. To be clear, I'm happy to have a discussion about value, but that is something separate and distinct from cost. Cost is what you pay; value is what you (hopefully) get in return. The issues depicted in the above illustrations show just how much "unpredictable return" is needed to overcome higher costs.

All of this reminds me of a famous line of Oscar Wilde's, from his play *Lady Windermere's Fan*, about what a cynic is: "A man who knows the cost of everything and the value of nothing." Similarly, British comedian John Oliver, in a segment about retirement plans on his show *Last Week Tonight*, told viewers to "think of fees like termites: They're tiny, they're barely noticeable, and they eat away at your [...] future." I would add that any advisor who talks about the value of advice and/or the value of relatively more expensive products without at least being equally clear about the importance of cost is being less than forthright. STANDUP advisors don't confuse the concepts of cost and value, and they make reasonable efforts to disclose both.

CHAPTER 11
NECESSARY DISCLOSURE

Why are any advisors afraid to discuss how and how much they get paid? It's ironic, given that their clients have already "gone first" in this personal disclosure about all the major financial things in their lives.

Theories abound, but my view is that the simplest reason for this curiosity may be a fear of the unknown. Most people want to work with others in an upfront manner, but there's a feeling among many of them that consumers will recoil in horror once they find out how much financial advice really costs. Of course, if you have to hide how much you get paid to get people to pay you, you might be either charging too much or not delivering enough value.

For a generation, there has been a debate within the financial services industry about the appropriate level of disclosure and, as of July 15, 2016, we've taken a big step forward. That's the date when the latest regulatory reform—the Client Relationship Model, Phase 2 (CRM2)—came into effect. The compensation paid to advisors and their firms will now be expressly disclosed. In addition, client performance will also now be reported. There is no doubt that we are finally making strides regarding disclosure in Canada.

It's about time. A recent study showed that 31% of a sample of 1,000 people working with an advisor thought they weren't paying anything for the advice they are getting.[27] Separate studies have shown that about two-thirds of investors don't know how much they are paying. The industry is belatedly moving toward avoiding and managing conflicts, and in this instance, "avoiding conflicts" may essentially be code for banning embedded compensation.

The debate has begun moving beyond what to disclose and into whether disclosure alone is enough. In late June 2016, the Canadian Securities Administrators (CSA), a collective of all the provincial and territorial securities commissions across the country, issued a statement indicating their intention to release a concept paper to look at eliminating embedded compensation altogether. After more than a generation since the first recommendation from the Ontario Securities Commission (OSC) to ban trailing commissions, the CSA is now willing to consider doing it. In short, it seems likely that we'll soon be moving from disclosure to disintermediation. However, if history is any guide, people who are eager for reform should not be holding their breath in anticipation.

Depending on how this progresses, it is possible that the "D" in STANDUP will ultimately no longer stand for "disclosure" but rather for "disintermediation." An outright ban on trailing commissions might eventually be enacted, forcing advisors and their firms to bill their clients in a more direct and transparent manner.

Moving from disclosure to disintermediation is interesting because some people like to quip that disclosure doesn't actually build trust, that it simply itemizes the reasons why a client shouldn't trust an advisor. The only real way to build trust is to avoid conflicts in the first place. Avoiding (as opposed to managing) conflicts means eliminating the embedded compensation that causes the conflict. Some would advocate having product suppliers modify embedded compensation so that it is agnostic to product placement, but I don't think that would work. The only reasonable way to overcome the problem of discount brokerages receiving trailing commissions is to stop paying trailing commissions altogether.

Who Wants Transparency?

Perhaps the easiest way to explain this is to look at how advisors might be paid using alternative business models. In the world of insurance, advisors basically work on commission at all times and split their earnings with their employers. Their employers cover all the associated costs (rent, staff, etc.). In the securities world through the Investment Industry Regulatory Organization of Canada (IIROC) and the mutual fund world through the Mutual Fund Dealers Association of Canada (MFDA), however, there are options regarding payout models.

The dominant model in the insurance and securities

structures allows advisors to be deemed employees. As such, advisors get to keep only a set percentage of the revenue they generate. The employee model might pay as little as 20% (very low revenue practices) to slightly over 50% (very high revenue practices).

The other model is the agency model, where the advisor works as an independent contractor for a higher percentage of the total revenue, but they pay all additional expenses (staff, rent, postage, etc.) out of pocket. The agency model usually pays the advisor at a flat percentage (typically 70% or 80% of total revenue) but leaves virtually all expenses for the advisor to pay personally. There are those who call this model the "entrepreneurial model" since it forces the advisor to think like a small business owner by paying careful attention to all expenses.

Having a strong entrepreneurial streak in them, many advisors clearly understand that costs matter when running their own practices. Whether it's rent, computer software and hardware, office supplies, or online access, advisors are certainly minding their Ps and Qs. Advisors want their firms to give them the latitude to do everything in their power to control costs and maximize net profits. They also want their firms to provide statements showing exactly how much each line item expense actually costs so they can better monitor things. These advisors are acting the way any other responsible small business owner would.

One way or another, advisor revenue depends on client performance, and some advisors would likely justify their use of pricier products through their expectation that ultimate returns will justify the higher costs. Still, cost-consciousness is conspicuously one-sided. One could say that that these advisors are more focused on revenues than on controlling client costs. Do as I say, not as I do.

Many advisors say they resist unbundling because they would make the same amount of money and the client would pay the same amount of money either way. That would be fine if that were what would actually happen, but that's not necessarily the case. With unbundling, clients could easily substitute expensive products with cheaper ones and pocket the difference. If this were to happen, the advisor's compensation wouldn't change, but client costs certainly would! In fact, there would likely be an arbitrage opportunity, where a saving (let's call it 1%) could be split between an advisor and a client. Perhaps an advisor should be paid 0.2% more. Even if this were to happen, a typical client could still save 0.8% and be substantially better off as a result by simply using products that cost 1% less.

Although advisors need and deserve to be paid, consumers also deserve to know what they're paying and what services they can reasonably expect in return. In this regard, it's like anything else: An informed consumer is a good consumer. Just as with cars, cribs, and health supplements, the more consumers know about products, the better their decisions. Here are four primary ways that an advisor might be paid:

1. An advisory arrangement: the advisor charges transparent, asset-based fees
2. A professional arrangement: the advisor charges hourly fees for deliverables
3. A sales representative arrangement: the advisor sells a product and receives a commission
4. An employee arrangement: the advisor gets a salary with a possible bonus (the dominant model in Canadian bank branches)

There are circumstances that legitimize each of these arrangements, and good disclosure leads to even better consumer decision-making. With the first two arrangements, clients receive invoices and pay directly (paying applicable sales taxes), and so that they know exactly how much they are paying their advisor. With the final two arrangements, however, the lack of a separate bill, or even a separate line item on a statement, could lead to clients making less than fully informed decisions. As such, the people who should want better disclosure are those currently working with advisors who use arrangements 3 and 4. In all cases, better disclosure leads to better advisor-client relationships.

What's an Appropriate Level of Disclosure?
Meaningful disclosure is vital. For a generation, cost and compensation disclosures appeared in bulky prospectuses filled with legal jargon. It is well documented that most prospectuses were never read—much less understood—for this very reason. Nonetheless,

people in the industry could honestly claim that they made disclosures. Technically, they would be correct. Practically speaking, the majority of investors still had no idea what they paid advisors.

The more clients understand what advisors do—and why—the more likely they will buy into the advice they receive. Furthermore, informed consent is widely seen as being a hallmark of any professional relationship. Where the person giving the advice has technical expertise that goes beyond what an ordinary person might reasonably be expected to know, it is only normal to expect a fair and balanced depiction of material considerations.

Think of cigarettes and the link to cancer. Although this causality is generally accepted today, it was not always the case. When the evidence began to show up in research papers, there were significant members of the medical community whose first reactions were denial. Suppose you were a physician in the 1950s who did not discourage cigarette smoking. In fact, suppose you actively encouraged it (as some did) as a benign means of relaxation. As time goes on, evidence mounts that your position is incorrect. As opinions evolve as people accept the evidence, should you continue to cling to your position?

The dilemma that professional physicians faced was one of grave consequence. As the primary advisors regarding their patients' health and welfare, they had an obligation to inform patients of any material risks associated with the consumption of the product. On the other hand, the evidence (in the early days at least) was not definitive, and there was a professional reputation to protect. What should professional, client-centred physicians have done? Should they have raised concerns when the evidence started to come out or only once the scientific community developed a sufficient body of evidence?

What about issues such as climate change? Almost all scientists are now thoroughly compelled by the evidence. Given the actions that governments around the world are now taking, surely there must be some need to tell people about the risks and why they are important. Many people would rather endure an unfortunate false positive or two if it meant that extra caution prevented or at least better managed the consequences associated with taking no action at all.

The idea of being a professional STANDUP advisor is supported by the twin pillars of research, which should be dispassionate and rigorous, and disclosure, which many feel should be compulsory. One pillar is never enough. Physicians learned this firsthand a generation or two ago. Those who tried to deny the evidence were ultimately seen, with the benefit of hindsight, as being less than professional.

Accepting that the social sciences always allow for at least some uncertainty, most reasonable people would be comfortable saying that the carcinogenic impact of cigarettes is now a generally accepted fact. Looking back on the past half-century, it should be obvious that the medical profession could have been more forthcoming about the harmful effects of cigarette smoke. Have we learned? Given that most people agree that more should have been done to alert the general population sooner, what has society decided regarding the proper role of professional intermediaries such as physicians? Is mere disclosure even enough, or were physicians, through their adherence to the Hippocratic Oath, expected to actively engage in the constructive modification of their patients' habits? It comes down to what we consider to be material.

How exactly might we define the word *material*—as in "advisors must always disclose all material facts"—when making recommendations? Synonyms include words such as *relevant*, *substantial*, and *pertinent*. It might be fair to say that any information that causes a person to change their opinion or behaviour is material. For example, if you had a sweet tooth and someone told you that sugar causes diabetes and weight gain, this information would be material if it caused you to change your habits. Otherwise, it would be interesting. Obviously, this information could be *relevant*, *substantial*, and *pertinent* whether you reduce your sugar intake or not, but to most people, changing one's behaviour is a pretty reliable sign of genuine materiality.

For many years now, it has been clear that disclosure is a significant contributor to consumer decision-making and can be used to manipulate choices. It bears repeating that "probable" does not mean "certain." One could pursue a course of action that is likely to yield superior results and still be worse off as a result of this attempt. Similarly, one could choose a course of action where an improbable outcome nonetheless bears fruit. The larger issue revolves around the concept of informed consent. Think about references in previous chapters to the professions and to the role of behavioural finance.

If you disclose information regarding one approach or product but not another, can a consumer really make an informed decision about which way to go? Using the impact of cost as an example, is the difference material at 0.1%? At 0.5%? At 1.0%? Where exactly is the threshold for materiality?

Tying this to Chapter 6, which discusses facts versus opinions, it should be obvious that, in principle at least, advisors should disclose all major facts so that clients can make an informed decision and advisors should disclaim all personal opinions so that clients can at least recognize them as opinions. As it now stands, most people can't tell the difference between fact and opinion because the usual explanations don't really distinguish between the two.

A critical aspect of professionalism is that practitioners do not impose their personal views on others. Instead, they work collaboratively and in a manner that the client believes is in their best interests. Obviously, different people may look at the same information and come to different conclusions, but any professional offering advice based on information that the client either does not fully understand or has not fully agreed with should probably disclose those details in a manner that allows the client to make an informed choice.

It would be disingenuous of any professional advisor not to at least portray all possible interpretations and alternatives fairly. Advisors are allowed to—and indeed expected to—advocate for one position over another, but they should do so only after giving all viewpoints a fair hearing. Again, people are allowed their own opinions, but they are not allowed their own facts.

Make It Meaningful

In order to do any good, disclosure needs to accurately depict not only what things are but also what they mean. Here's a simple way of looking at it. If an advisor makes a disclosure, but the client doesn't understand what the advisor said or wrote, then informed consent may still not be present, even though disclosures were made and concepts were explained. That's a huge problem.

When this happens, the advisor can say something like, "I absolutely told the client about this." While that sort of statement would certainly be true as far as it goes, it wouldn't exactly provide evidence that the client had "bought in" to the advisor's recommendation. The fancy word that lawyers and regulators like to use is *saliency*—does the information stand out prominently so that the person seeing, reading, or hearing it understands what it means and what the implications are?

One such depiction might be simple one-year return expectations (value propositions) associated with competing products in the same asset class, where that asset class (a stock market of some kind) has an expected return of 8%. The depictions below show that an average investor's expected return is the return of the asset class benchmark minus the cost of the product, plus or minus an expected degree of variance. This is exactly what the Sharpe paper referenced in Chapter 6 means in practical terms.

In these illustrations, Graph A (for alpha) features a 6.5% average expected return, with a far larger range, while Graph B (for beta) features a 7.5% average expected return with a relatively modest range. The reason for these numbers is that the assumed average management expense ratio (MER) for an F-class actively managed product is 1.5%, and the assumed MER for an F-class passively managed product is 0.5%. In short, the overall outcome differences are due to differing product costs and the likely dispersion of returns associated with differing value propositions.

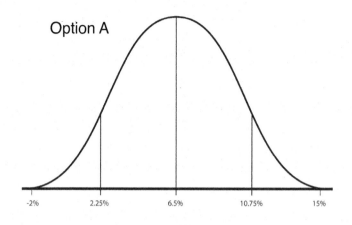

Option A

| -2% | 2.25% | 6.5% | 10.75% | 15% |

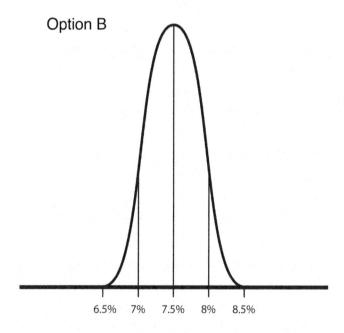

Option B

| 6.5% | 7% | 7.5% | 8% | 8.5% |

I should explain that these graphs are simple statistical concepts in an abstract sense. They are merely illustrations to explain a conceptual trade-off between competing alternatives. There is no data that supports the notion that such distributions occur as actual events.

Graph A shows expectations for products that cost more, and it also features a greater variance of possible return outcomes due to active security selection. Meanwhile, Graph B is more or less hugging the benchmark minus a lower cost. One would reasonably expect a modest tracking error for the passive option and a much higher variance for the active option.

So is it worth a *certain* 1.0% cost increase if that choice might involve a similar reduction in long-term expected returns with a wider dispersion of outcomes? Remember that this is a one-year proposition. You could multiply this decision by the number of years in your time horizon to get a more meaningful feel for what's at stake. Remember that for every person on the right side of the centre line in either option, there's another person on the left side. There are pros and cons to both approaches, and both options have a constituency. Which option is a typical investor more likely to choose if given the choice? How many are actually given the choice?

A question I like to ask is, "If I could show you how to save tens or even hundreds of thousands of dollars over the course of your lifetime by simply replacing your current investment products with products that have a similar expected pre-cost risk and return profile but which cost 1% less and have less expected year-over-year volatility relative to their benchmark, is that something that would interest you?" Almost every time I ask it, I get a resounding "Yes!"

The concern is not about which option the client chooses but in being clear that the client understands the trade-offs involved with the competing choices. Investors should always understand their options. While regulators have finally made meaningful and transparent disclosure now a precondition of all account-opening procedures, many feel that more needs to be done.

For years now, STANDUP advisors have been voluntarily doing similar things to improve professionalism, trust, and understanding. Truly effective disclosure should be written in terms any competent layperson could understand. Client sign-off regarding advisor compensation is now mandatory. It is not required for the other considerations. Additional disclosures might include the use of additional one-page documents for letters of engagement and the like.

With client sign-off, clients cannot say certain details were not set out clearly at the beginning. This has potential benefits for everyone. Firms should like it because having the client sign-off can make it harder for them to sue compliant advisors. Consumers and advisors should like it, too, because setting out the terms of any engagement should enhance the level of accountability, understanding, and trust for both parties since everyone has an obligation to do better.

Here's another example based on an article written by Christopher Davis of Morningstar in the summer of 2016. We can see how a simple depiction of "what is" (i.e., how much of your total return is eaten up by an

MER in any given year) might be incomplete and/or misleading.[28] A more meaningful (salient) depiction might show not only the annual costs but also the long-term impact of those costs.

Note how matter of fact the information is when depicted as a percentage of a historical return:

A great value? Fees eat more than 25% of an 8% market return

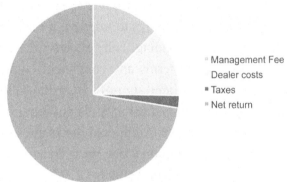

- Management Fee
  Dealer costs
- Taxes
- Net return

Source: Morningstar. Chart assumes 8% gross annual return and 2.2% iin annual expesnes.

Now look at the same cost structure when applied to a reasonable return expectation:

A great value? Fees eat up nearly 45% of a 5% market return

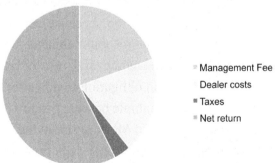

- Management Fee
  Dealer costs
- Taxes
- Net return

Source: Morningstar. Chart assumes 5% gross annual return and 2.2% in annual expenses.

Finally, let's look at the impact of those costs (using the historical data) over a long time frame:

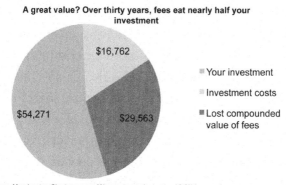

A great value? Over thirty years, fees eat nearly half your investment

$16,762

$54,271

$29,563

▪ Your investment
▪ Investment costs
▪ Lost compounded value of fees

Source: Morningstar. Chart assumes 8% gross annual return and 2.2% in annual expenses.

The Cigarettes of Our Generation

Perhaps the biggest challenge in the financial services industry is the issue of giving responsible advice. What role should a qualified advisor play? When the class-action lawsuits started in the tobacco industry, they targeted the tobacco companies (i.e., the product manufacturers) for making harmful products without disclosing the material risks associated with their consumption. The physicians (i.e., the professional, advice-giving intermediaries) were typically spared from lawsuits because they were seen as mere conduits and not the root of the problem. Besides, the product manufacturers had deeper pockets. If this precedent holds, then evidence linking higher product costs and weaker long-term performance could add significantly to corporate liability.

With tobacco, legislators ultimately came to conclude that the welfare of the citizenry trumped the right of corporations to make profits, and they forced the disclosure on the tobacco industry. The objective of recent reforms in the financial services industry is to make the cost of investing—both the cost of the advice *and* the cost of the products—clearer so consumers can make decisions based on more meaningful inputs.

Rebecca Cowdery, a securities lawyer with Borden Ladner Gervais LLP, agrees that product cost should be part of the picture, too, but has concerns about operational issues. She had this to say:

> I think this expanded disclosure is a huge missing piece of what investors need to know about the full amount of the cost of investing, but it would certainly include a fair amount of transition and a lot of work on the investment dealers' part to report it accurately.[29]

The cost of advice will soon be appearing on all client statements. If governmental protection is indeed what is required, and if our legislators are genuinely interested in consumers making better financial decisions, then bolder product cost disclosures might also be around the corner.

Calibrating Disclosure

The financial services industry is still looking for the "Goldilocks" level of disclosure: not too much, not too little. How much is required before making a decision anyway? It should be added that disclosure doesn't have to be only about compensation and cost either. For instance, at the time of account opening, it would likely be helpful to make more meaningful disclosures about volatility (some people call this risk, others call it standard deviation), expected returns, and risk classifications in general.

A couple of things are now moving to the forefront of the industry: 1) the value propositions of certain financial products, and 2) the prices associated with both products and financial advice. I would suggest that most consumers cannot do a reasonable job of explaining what investment products cost or how much of that cost (if any) goes to the advisor.

We've looked at the debate between cheaper passive products and more expensive active ones, but our first examination revolved around broad evidence on the topic of relative performance. What about the related question of value? I find it interesting whenever I have this conversation with other advisors. When I ask them about cost, most advisors quickly, seamlessly, and subtly change the subject and talk about value instead. There's a difference. Cost is clear and quantifiable; value is less clear and very much in the eye of the beholder.

I suspect the conversation is the same with clients, too. For instance, there might be two products that have a similar mandate and benchmark (e.g., both might invest in Canadian large company stocks). One product (perhaps an actively managed F-class mutual fund) might cost 1.25%. The other (perhaps a passively managed ETF) might cost 0.25%. The difference in cost is 1%, and if nothing else changes, the cheaper product should perform better over time because paying 1.0% less in cost means getting 1.0% more in return. The factual difference in cost cannot be disputed; the subjective difference in value is an open question. The question being, will the more expensive F-class product outperform the cheaper alternative by enough to justify the added cost? I suspect this is unlikely to happen consistently.

I can't begin to tell you how many advisors say something like, "I recommend the active product because it is the only one that offers clients the opportunity to beat the benchmark." While that is certainly true, I still haven't met a single advisor who then goes on to say, "Of course, using an active strategy also means that the client might lag the benchmark by considerably more than the product cost."

We all need to recognize that cost (what you pay) and value (what you get in return) are different things. In the example above, the difference in cost is unambiguously 1.0%. The difference in value could be massive—in either direction. The passive option could outperform by 3.0% or more; the active option could outperform by 3.0% or more. Price is just the conspicuous and easily quantified portion of the value proposition.

Value is a fair and important consideration, but it

doesn't excuse anyone from skipping the question of cost altogether. It is simply impossible to have a meaningful discussion about value if you do not, at the very least, quantify cost. In my opinion, that's a huge part of what is wrong about the financial services industry today. The industry is so busy talking about perceived value that most consumers never think to ask about price. There's a saying that price is only an issue when value is in question. Most people apply the saying to financial advice, but in my opinion, it is far more applicable to financial products.

Think of the last time you bought a car. Did the sales representative talk about price or value, or was there at least a balanced conversation about both? Let's say you're going for a test drive. The sales rep says the car has 300 horsepower (value). He says it has heated seats and airbags for both front seats (value). Curious, you ask him how much the car costs and expect him to tell you without hesitation.

In any other circumstance, when someone offers you advice about something yet avoids questions about price, you're likely to get suspicious of that person's motives. Investing is perhaps the only industry in the world where the cheapest products are generally the best, yet it is also an industry where many consumers seem very interested in bells and whistles while showing little concern for price. To make matters worse, our regulators have taken a generation to force transparency on the industry through the disclosure of the compensation paid to advisors and their firms. To this day, other than a single, modest reference in the "fund facts" or "ETF facts" document you're likely to get when you first buy a product, there are no comparable disclosures of product cost on client statements whatsoever.

Let's put that in perspective using a moderately priced mutual fund with an MER of 2.3%. Let's say you have $200,000 as your investment and that you hold your portfolio for forty years. You'd be paying $4,600 a year in total cost (the MER includes both the cost of the underlying product as well as the cost of all advice)—for forty years. That's $184,000!

At the beginning of this chapter, I suggested that the "D" in STANDUP might soon be repurposed and that instead of it standing for "disclosure," it might soon come to stand for "disintermediation." Other jurisdictions outside of Canada have concluded that disclosure in and of itself simply doesn't do enough to protect the public. For instance, Martin Wheatley, former head of the Financial Conduct Authority (FCA), the financial market regulator in the UK, acknowledged that disclosure doesn't do enough to protect investors. Greg Medcraft of the Australian Securities and Investments Commission (ASIC) goes one step further. He says disclosure is largely a "waste of time" because no one (apart from lawyers) actually reads it.[30] The UK and Australia have already banned embedded compensation.

I agree. The system needs to be reformed. Furthermore, since the integrity of the entire financial services industry could be called into question, it now seems as though finding an honourable way to leave the world of embedded compensation is the top priority.

CHAPTER 12
EMBEDDED COMPENSATION CAUSES BIAS

There are two primary types of bias that might exist in the financial services industry: 1) a bias in favour of active products over passive ones, and 2) a bias in favour of embedded compensation products over unbundled products. In many instances, this is the same problem, since many active products are available primarily with embedded compensation, and virtually all passive products are available without embedded compensation. Having already discussed the active/passive situation at length, we now need to focus on alternative compensation structures.

The lack of meaningful alternatives (i.e., passive embedded-compensation products) makes for an interesting circumstance. The easy availability of embedded structures may be the reason why so many advisors profess to favour active management yet nonetheless refuse to recommend some of the most highly respected mutual funds available. Companies such as PH&N, Mawer, Chou, Steadyhand, and Beutel Goodman offer reputable actively managed products but pay little or nothing in trailing commissions. Active or not, a lack of embedded compensation can lead to a lack of shelf space with most advisors. I've often wondered what portfolios would look like if passive options paid trailing commissions but active ones did not.

Our challenge is to eliminate all forms of bias so that advisors' motives cannot be called into question. The obvious solution is to create a level playing field. There is an equally obvious way of doing that: Simply have all products pay advisors the same. Ultimately, an advisor's preferred way of getting paid should not influence product recommendations. There are two ways of meeting this objective of consistency; either

1. increase/decrease the compensation on passive products by bringing it to the level paid on active ones as may be applicable, or

2. decrease/increase the compensation on active products by bringing it to the level paid on passive ones as may be applicable.

When it comes to eliminating bias, either option would work. When it comes to doing what's right for the client, however, the second option is clearly more appropriate.

Anyone who wishes to work without the input of an advisor should be allowed to do so without having to pay for that decision. However, many observers believe that most people would be better off working with an advisor.

The other concern is overall product cost, which, to my mind, is the real issue in all of this. There is increasing evidence indicating that advisors and regulators alike have not done a good job of explaining the importance of cost to investors. Cost matters…a lot. To make this point abundantly clear, here's what ETF analyst Eric Balchunas of Bloomberg had to say:

> The whole story of the big sea change underway in money management isn't necessarily from mutual funds into exchange-traded funds or active to passive or human to robo-advisor—it's really about high-cost to low-cost.[31]

What Are "Trailers"?

It never ceases to amaze me that an industry as sophisticated and tightly regulated as financial services still can't reconcile what it is with what it purports to be. For instance, many products, including mutual funds, offer "trailers" to advisors on their products. The question is, what are trailers? More specifically, are they commissions or fees?

Many think this is a question of simple semantics and dismiss it. I think it's more than that. We should be able to come to a clear conclusion about whether trailers are one or the other, and to my mind, this is easy to resolve. Section 3.2 of Regulation 81-105 defines them as "trailing commissions." This regulatory definition extends to all IIROC (securities) and MFDA (mutual fund) firms. The Canada Revenue Agency

(CRA) has provided a resolution. The CRA says trailers are commissions.

If you're still not persuaded, feel free to consult a handy dictionary. I've consulted a few, and although the definitions vary slightly, the general consensus is that fees are paid for services rendered and commissions are paid for products placed. It should be obvious that trailers are commissions.

When running an ad about a product that pays trailers, advisors are required to run a disclaimer stating that commissions including trailing commissions might be associated with the products in question. Conversely, I've seen dozens of articles in the press where someone in the business refers to trailers as fees. In my opinion, this terminology selectivity is another form of investment porn.

What about the representatives of the firms that manufacture the products that pay those trailers? As far as I can tell, what constitutes a trailer seems to depend almost entirely on who's doing the talking. If it's mentioned in an ad, prospectus, or "fund facts" document, the trailer is a commission. If it's being discussed with a retail client or in the popular media, the trailer is a fee. Trailers seem to be shape-shifters. How can something be an apple to one audience and an orange to another? Think back to Chapter 6, which discusses facts versus opinions. You might say that trailers are fees in the opinion of some and that trailers are commissions in the opinion of others, but that's not the issue. Disagreement about terminology isn't that bad. In fact, disagreement can be healthy if it allows for a healthy exchange of ideas. What should not be acceptable, ever, is the misrepresentation of a product's basic character based strictly on who is doing the talking or who is doing the listening. You can see why certain people might wish to mischaracterize commissions as fees. Sales representatives earn commissions; professionals charge fees. How can anyone credibly present oneself as a non-sales professional while working on commission?

Terminology, consistency, and precision are vitally important. Mutual funds and the trailing commissions they often pay have been around for almost thirty years in Canada, and the people who use them still cannot come up with a clear and consistent message to depict their true character. Virtually every mutual fund company in the country refers to trailers as commissions in their formal correspondence to the public, yet when they correspond with advisors or comment to the media, they switch to calling them fees.

Stated differently, this is not a matter of some people using one term and others disagreeing and using another. This is a clear, repeated, industry-wide manipulation of terminology where the same speakers (sometimes fund companies, sometimes advisors) refer to the exact same things as something different depending on who they are talking to.

Advisor Bias

The debate has raged for a generation. What, if anything, should be done about embedded compensation?

For over twenty years, the pro-embedded camp insisted that embedded compensation did not likely cause bias, as no one had produced a peer-reviewed study to demonstrate that it did. Of course, no one had done a rigorous study looking at actual fund flows on the subject, so no one really knew anything for sure.

That changed in 2015, when the Canadian Securities Administrators (CSA) published two papers, one a literature review by the consulting firm Brondesbury Group, the other an impact study led by York University professor Douglas Cumming. The Brondesbury Group review verified that several peer-reviewed articles had indeed demonstrated advisor bias as a result of embedded compensation. The Cumming report, meanwhile, looked at real-world fund data to confirm essentially the same thing. In other words, we now have evidence of something that the industry insisted did not exist. That alone should bring us to the conclusion that wholesale change is necessary.

As is typical of regulators, who have a government-sanctioned public interest mandate, they released a policy paper for public comment on the subject. They put out a policy paper, left it open for interested parties to comment on for 120 days, and then reported on what they heard at a later date. Their press release indicated a desire to explore the likely effects of a potential ban on embedded compensation. As you might expect, the people who want to retain the embedded-compensation structure went into full defence mode. In trying to discern the best course of action to protect ordinary investors, it should be obvious that when a group that calls itself the Financial Advisors Association of Canada (Advocis) weighs in, it will likely advocate for the benefit of financial advisors.

Stakeholders such as Advocis began an extensive public relations campaign but made no mention of their previous position claiming that embedded compensation did not cause bias. Their public comments to the media were all about client choice and access to advice. I've often wondered how people would react if Advocis combined the Cumming evidence with their own logic. How would you respond to someone who urged you to choose potentially biased advice? If the interests of advisors and the interests of ordinary investors are not aligned, would you trust the advisor lobby to offer a balanced viewpoint?

In the recent past, countries such as the UK and Australia banned embedded compensation. In some instances, these bans were part of even larger, more sweeping reforms. In the UK, a component of the legislated reform was a significant ramping up of the demonstrated proficiency of registrants. Existing advisors would need to pass rigorous tests to stay in business.

Shortly after reforms were enacted in the UK, the advisor population dropped by about 25%. To hear the pro-embedded camp tell it, the sole reason for the drop in advisor population was the newly minted ban on embedded compensation. This narrative was used even though it was almost universally agreed that many advisors were admitted into the industry when the barriers to entry were low. More meaningful proficiency exams have since been introduced. Unfortunately, no one can prove what their collective motives were, so the debate cannot be resolved. All that we know for certain is that a large segment of the advisor population left the business. Call it "causation scapegoating" leading to plausible deniability.

The Imaginary Advice Gap

The obvious extension to the argument against banning trailers is that if something similar were to happen in Canada, we'd lose about one quarter of all advisors. This might lead some to suggest that there could be tens of thousands—perhaps even hundreds of thousands—of Canadian investors who would be left with no access to qualified advice. Perhaps. I am highly doubtful, personally.

Technically, no one knows for sure how this will play out—either in terms of what will be enacted and when, or in terms of what the impact will ultimately be. With that out of the way, however, we can look at some additional evidence to get a good sense of what is likely in store.

We all know that in a court of law, people giving evidence are asked to tell the truth, the whole truth, and nothing but the truth. It is in the "whole truth" part where the defenders of the way things are currently done are so deficient. How can we trust people to guide us if they won't even tell us the whole story when we go to them seeking balanced counsel?

Study after study and poll after poll have clearly established that many investors have absolutely no idea how or how much they are paying for financial advice. The reforms contemplated through the Client Relationship Model, Phase 2 (CRM2) might make things better, but the experiences of other jurisdictions (again, the UK and Australia) show us that disclosure by itself doesn't really work in managing advisor-client conflicts.

Many arguments have been made on this subject. Here are my responses to the most prominent ones:

Argument: "There should be as much choice in the system as possible; taking the option of paying via embedded compensation robs clients of an established choice."

Response: Embedded compensation that has differential compensation is not a viable choice because it does not eliminate advisor bias. Retaining suboptimal choices does not lead to better investor outcomes.

Argument: "A major drop in the absolute number of advisors would cause an 'advice gap' in Canada."

Response: Watch what you're measuring. An

"advice gap" only occurs when there are people who want, need, and are willing to pay for advice but cannot find an advisor. An advice gap is measured by the number of people who fit all of those criteria, not by the number of advisors no longer in business. Even if the advisor population were to drop moderately, the concern may be overblown because of the following:

- Smaller investors would have the option of working with bank branches or robo-advisors.
- The advisors remaining in the industry might be glad to take on more clients.
- Some investors could choose to become DIY investors to save on advisory costs

We need to take these points (and possibly others) into consideration for there be a meaningful assessment of whether or not an advice gap will occur.

Argument: "Small clients cannot afford to pay separately for advice."

Response: Small clients have already been paying for advice through trailing commissions. Paying for advice separately and transparently has no impact on the cost of the advice (assuming the advisor charges the same amount either way). Transparency has no impact on affordability.

The Value Gap

Insisting that clients pay separately for financial advice will not *create an advice gap*, but it could very easily *expose a value gap*. As noted previously, many people who work with an advisor who recommends mutual funds have no idea of how and how much their advisor is paid. Even those who understand the "how" part consistently underestimate the "how much" part by a significant margin.

Once ordinary people are confronted with the substantial costs associated with financial advice, they will (in some instances for the first time ever) be able to do their own intuitive cost/benefit analysis: "What am I paying…and what am I getting in return?" If, in doing this analysis, people decide to either work with robo-advisors or serve as their own advisor, it is a decision they will make in full awareness of the cost of advice. Choosing to forego that traditional form of advice is not an example of a gap being created; it is evidence of someone making an informed decision.

In my view, the solution is simple. We need to end embedded compensation at the first opportunity because embedded compensation in its current format causes bias that harms investors. Retail investors deserve purposeful solutions to the problems that can arise from embedded compensation.

The Final Frontier

Over the past several years, I've spoken to representatives at a number of advisory firms about their philosophies so I could get a sense of their values and corporate culture. My sense is that compensation models can go a long way in explaining (or at least predicting) belief systems. Companies will say their advisors can work using either transactional or buy-and-hold philosophies. Either way, there's room. They say you can be a comprehensive planner or a simple investment specialist. Either way, there's room for that too. The advisors can be commission-based or fee-based. Either way, they would be welcomed.

We should explore and discuss differences of opinion rationally. Over the past few generations, we've seen a few hotly contested societal debates on civil rights issues such as same-sex marriage, universal suffrage, and racial integration. There have also been heated debates regarding science and technology. Ongoing debates of this kind include topics such as climate change and renewable energy. Perhaps the debate regarding the appropriateness of embedded compensation is the financial services debate of our generation. One thing to note about these kinds of debates is that a generation or two after they occur, people generally look back and marvel at the fact that there were actually people out there resisting change. For example, the history books have not been kind to those who favoured apartheid.

Let's say a client is fully invested in a mutual fund

portfolio with an average management expense ratio (MER) of 2.54%. Remember that an MER is the annual cost of owning the fund and that the results you get are reported after those charges have been deducted from the investor's performance.

The cost (MER) on an A-class fund might break down like this:

Product overhead (administration):	0.25%
Fund manager charges (including profit):	1.00%
Trailing commission	
(split between advisor and firm):	1.00%
Total:	2.25%

The first thing you should understand is that mutual funds might be the only products in the country that are advertised with taxes included, such as the Harmonized Sales Tax (HST) in Ontario and Atlantic Canada or the Goods and Services Tax (GST) elsewhere in Canada. For example, 1.99% pre-tax cost + 13% HST is 2.25% total cost.

Currently, there are three primary ways that an advisor selling mutual funds gets paid: 1) a deferred sales charge (DSC), 2) front end (FE) 0%, or 3) separately using an F-class version of the fund. We need to recognize that investors are buying the same fund with different compensation structures. The underlying investments, manager, sponsor, objectives, and other major attributes are the same. The only difference is how the client is billed and, as a result, how the advisor and their firm are paid.

Deferred Sales Charge (DSC)

The letters "DSC" still appear on many client statements, and when I see them, I ask would-be clients if they know what those letters mean. Most do not. A deferred sales charge (DSC) is commonly referred to as a "back-end load."

For most stock-based mutual funds, it means the advisor and their firm get a 5.0% commission within a couple of days of the sale and an additional 0.5% annually (0.125% quarterly) for as long as the investor holds the account. The numbers are similar, but lower, on income funds.

The investor now has a potential charge that can be worked off over time. Note that an investor can change from one fund to another in the same fund family at any time. Although some advisors charge up to 2.0% for this right, most do not charge anything provided clients do this infrequently. It should be noted that clients can always withdraw up to 10% invested annually with no penalties. The 10% number is not cumulative, however, so one cannot withdraw 0% one year and expect to be able to withdraw more than 10% the next year without penalty. When it comes to the 10% rule, the words "use it or lose it" apply.

As you might imagine, mutual fund companies don't like losing money. If they pay an advisor and their firm $5,000 (5.0% on a hypothetical $100,000 invested) in week one, they're not going to be happy if you pull your money out in week three. In fact, they'd be out about $5,000. The charge is supposed to act as a disincentive to selling early. The actual amount charged drops over time, since fund companies can earn out their prepaid advisory costs in the form of ongoing fees over time. A DSC redemption schedule might look something like this:

Year	Charge
1	5.5%
2	5.0%
3	4.5%
4	4.0%
5	3.0%
6	2.0%
7	1.0%
Thereafter	No charge

To put this in perspective, if you had $50,000 invested in a DSC fund and elected to redeem everything in year two, your charge would be $2,250 (5.0% of $50,000 less 10% that can be redeemed for free). From a disclosure perspective, this is a charge over and above the MER, but it is only incurred if there is a redemption of more than 10% in any given year prior to the schedule running its course.

The people at Morningstar have elected to suspend their awards gala for 2016 on the grounds that they give many of the prizes to companies and funds based on subjective data. The fact that they gave out Morningstar Awards based on "juried" selections did not make the ceremonies any more compliant. To their credit, Morningstar did not want to "feed the beast" of mutual fund marketing departments any longer.

At any rate, this is an important development because advisors using DSC funds could be armed with annual award data to assist in the sales process. Until now, advisors could use the awards to justify redeeming existing funds (including those with outstanding DSC balances) in order to place the proceeds into this year's winning funds, thereby earning a commission, starting the DSC period all over again for their valued clients, and possibly causing an avoidable capital gain.

Front End (FE) 0%

Front end (FE) 0% funds and DSC funds have identical MERs—typically a little under 2.5%. One thing that has become quite popular over the past decade or so is that advisors have been moving client assets from DSC to FE 0% once the DSC schedule (such as shown above) runs out and there are no transaction costs to the client to do so. Note that if this switch takes place in a traditional investment (i.e., non-registered) account, there could be tax consequences.

The 0% part of the FE format is really just a matter of taste. Advisors usually charge nothing to invest money on a front-end (sometimes called "no load") basis, but they are allowed to if they wish. Most do not charge to allow access to this format. Instead of getting a large commission up front, advisors and their firms get nothing up front but generally get more on an ongoing basis. Most stock funds pay a 1.0% annual trailing commission (0.25% quarterly) to advisors and their firms using the FE format and pay a 0.5% annual trailing commissions (0.125% quarterly) on income funds. The cost to the client is the exact same under both DSC and FE formats. Clients can sell FE funds at any time with no penalty.

F-Class

We'll talk a lot more about F-class funds in a later chapter, but for now, it might be helpful to think of them as FE funds with no trailers baked into the cost and no payment made to the advisor. In the example used above, an FE A-class fund that costs 2.53% would cost between 1.40% and 1.43% in an F-class format (stripping out both the 1% trailing commission while accounting for how the HST liability is managed).

Since F-class funds pay advisors nothing, it is up to advisors who use F-class funds to bill their clients directly. Obviously, if the advisor billed in an identical format, the same 0.25% + HST would be billed every quarter.

If you asked advisors to rate where their loyalty lies—with their employers and suppliers, their clients, or their own families—very few would place their employers and suppliers anywhere other than third place. So here's the obvious win here for everyone except those who finish third in this little prioritization thought experiment: What if the advisor charged a little more, used products that cost a lot less, and then passed the net savings on to clients?

How things are now: the client pays a ~2.5% MER, and the advisor's firm gets 1.0%

What-if scenario: the client pays a total of ~1.76% with products costing 0.4%, and the advisor's firm getting 1.2% while charging $0.156 in HST (the HST is 13% of the 1.2%)

In the what-if scenario, the client saves 0.74% less any tax inefficiency for HST. On $100,000, *that's $740 each and every year*. That's an annual saving for about one-third of total costs. The advisor, instead of being a "price taker" who gets paid only what suppliers will pay him, gets to earn a bit more (good advice costs money, you know) and increases their revenue by 20% *while doing what is right for the client, sourcing out cheaper products, and passing along the lion's share of the savings*. That's a clear win/win situation!

For fun, let's imagine the account was a truly large one—say, $1 million. For starters, the advisor would likely be delighted to work for 1.0%. Adding on the HST and an additional 0.4% product cost, we're now saving the client about 1.0%. For those of you keeping score at home, 1.0% of $1 million is $10,000. This is the amount the client would save every year for the rest of their life, unless, of course, the account grew over time. In that case, the client would save even more. This, of course, assumes everything else is the same and there is no incremental return added by the active management. Other things will not be the same but are about equally likely to be better or worse for both options.

Do Advisors Recommend Options with Unlikely Positive Outcomes?

Consistency is an important part of any undertaking, and people constantly look to professionals to offer consistent, impartial advice tailored to their circumstances. Someone with certain medical symptoms could visit three or four physicians and presumably get the same diagnosis each time. Qualified physicians take a dispassionate approach to medical advice.

Increasingly, advisors are talking as though they are professionals—but are they? More to the point, are the recommendations of advisors consistent, impartial, and rational? Surgeons are required to explain the pros and cons of various procedures to patients in terms that patients can understand, but the final decision rests with the patient, who will decide based on personal values, preferences, and the facts involved.

There is considerable evidence that the majority of actively managed mutual funds lag their benchmark and that the handful that outperform cannot be reliably identified before the fact. Furthermore, it seems the reason for this collective average shortcoming is cost. Using a high-cost strategy to try to beat the market is more likely than not to cause the person pursuing the strategy to fall short as a direct result of spending the money and making the effort.

Extending this logic, should a professional advisor recommend that a client take a trip to a casino and gamble with their life savings as a retirement strategy? Both scenarios feature the possibility of improbable but outsized returns. The metaphor isn't entirely appropriate because people at casinos lose at their own risk, but with more expensive actively managed products, investors will more likely feel the impact as an opportunity cost—a reduction in your long-term return versus the potential of losing everything in a casino. Accepting that there are risks associated with both activities, do the rewards offer fair compensation for the risks involved?

We all know that advisors would tell their clients that it's unwise to risk blowing their life's savings at a casino, but that's the point. At a minimum, advisors need to acknowledge that it's riskier to pursue expensive strategies that attempt to beat the market. They need to make sure that the client understands the risks before setting out. Both casinos and active investing strategies offer the small possibility of winning in exchange for some degree of risk. Note that the definition of *winning* can differ. One means "making money," the other means "doing better than available alternatives."

Reconciliation Time

All of this raises the question of why the industry has still not formulated a consistent and rational way to eliminate advisor bias. It's not really protecting consumers, either.

To make matters worse, consumers are still paying trailing commissions to discount brokerage firms where advice is neither requested nor received. This suits sales-oriented advisors very well because they can tell their clients that it "costs no more" to buy (A-class) mutual fund products from them than from a discount broker. I disagree. I think it's just another way of demonstrating that the advice from the people who say such things is worthless.

By paying firms that offer no advice (discount brokerages) the same as those who offer advice (advisory firms), product manufacturers send an implicit message that the advice being offered is worthless. STANDUP advisors are of the opinion that such a message debases the value of advice. They argue that cost is supposed to cover advice, wisdom, specialized knowledge, and guidance. At a discount brokerage, there is no advisor to offer any of this, but the embedded compensation persists anyway.

Investors would appreciate the value proposition of qualified advice far more if it were put out in the open where they could see what they are paying and have discussions about the value of what they are getting in return. Unbundling—the removal of all embedded compensation from all product offerings—would accomplish this quite nicely. After all, how can anyone determine the value of something if they don't know its cost?

Another way of looking at this is to consider that incentives can have unintended consequences. When articulating a unifying theme of their bestseller *Freakonomics,* authors Steven Levitt and Stephen Dubner said, "People respond to incentives." Incentives are neither good nor bad in and of themselves. However, in the case of trailing commissions, advisors have a potential incentive to recommend the products that pay trailers while systematically ignoring other products that are potentially just as good or better (and also considerably cheaper). Meanwhile, clients who rely on advisors for guidance are none the wiser about the biases that are baked into the system and add to the costs that diminish their returns.

CHAPTER 13

PARTS AND LABOUR SOLD SEPARATELY

The principle of the primacy of consumer interests is so entrenched that it applies to virtually all walks of life.

Let's look at auto mechanics. Pretend that we have a simple matrix regarding parts and labour. You can use quality replacement parts or cheap knock-offs as one decision, and you can install them yourself or hire a mechanic as another. Now let's pretend these variables are linked. What if your actual options were only twofold? What if you need to choose between quality parts you install at home by yourself and knock-off parts a mechanic installs for you at the garage? Which would you choose? The choice invites some implicit trade-offs between cost, quality, and convenience. Both options have benefits; both have drawbacks.

Think about this from a consumer's perspective, especially if that consumer is like me around a garage. I don't know a catalytic converter from a caliper. Imagine if a mechanic told customers that they would have to agree to use inferior knock-off parts if they wanted the work done at his garage. You can use quality parts if you do the work yourself, but you have to use knock-offs if you want someone else to do it for you. How would you feel if your mechanic gave you this option? Wouldn't your first question be: "Why can't I get the good parts and still pay the hourly rate to have you install them, Mr. Mechanic?" Indeed.

As a consumer, how would you feel about a biased system that leads to the recommendation of potentially inferior products? Shouldn't consumers be encouraged to choose products based on merit alone? The investment and insurance industries have long-standing rules and codes of ethics that address these issues.

The cardinal rule of the financial services industry is that the client comes first, and advisors are expected to subordinate their own interests to those of their clients. If a prospective client sees two or more advisors on a matter and receives conflicting advice, how should the client proceed? Provided the recommendations are reasonable, the client should consider each of them. The problem is that embedded compensation sets up a conflict of interest where advisors recommend only products that bill accordingly.

This might be a good time to stop and reflect upon the pro-embedded rallying cry of "client choice." If these groups are great champions of choice, why would they exclude certain choices? Certain groups have made considerable noise about their commitment to client choice. I would submit that they tend to define *choice* narrowly. To them, the choice is between embedded compensation and non-embedded compensation, and the competing options regarding the advisor's business model is the choice under consideration. Their discussion of the topic is incomplete, and their omissions are likely contrary to the public interest. Truth be told, there are at least three choices that clients need to consider:

1. Business model: embedded versus transparent compensation
2. Value proposition: low-cost versus high-cost products
3. Advisory relationship: non-discretionary versus discretionary

The thing that strikes me is the way the "proponents of choice" seem to ignore the second and third choices as if to suggest that those choices are of no consequence or do not exist. I can assure you that they are both of considerable consequence. My personal view is that the second and third choices are at least as important as the first one. But here's the irony: The so-called proponents of choice regarding the business model decision are effectively cutting off choices regarding both value propositions and advisory relationships when people choose to pay through embedded compensation based on current embedded-compensation structures. Like Henry Ford, who wrote, "Any customer can have a car painted any colour he wants so long as it is black," these folks seem to be saying, "Any client can work with me any way they want so long as they pay me an embedded compensation."

Here's a simple test you can do whenever you find

an advisor who steadfastly insists that the current debate is about client choice. Ask them how many (or perhaps what percentage) of their clients work with them using a format that *does not* involve embedded compensation. One would expect proponents of choice to have several clients using several different business models. My experience, in speaking with so-called pro-choice advisors is that they overwhelmingly favour embedded compensation. Speaking strictly from personal experience, I would go so far as to estimate that the vast majority of them have the vast majority of their clients' assets invested using an embedded format. These people are really just pro-embedded. They use the pro-choice approach to justify a format that they favour. Actions speak louder than words. Why not have some fun and ask a few "pro-choice" advisors to work with you using an unbundled format? My experience—with the exceptions so rare that they can literally be counted on one hand—is that "pro-choice" advisors are really just pro-embedded advisors.

In addition, we have spent much of the recent past discussing the desirability of moving to a "statutory best interests" (sometimes called "fiduciary") standard. It is impossible to earn commissions in a discretionary account. If an investor wanted their advisor to be a fiduciary, there would be no way if their advisor earned embedded commissions. Once again, the choice of business model precludes a vitally important option regarding a potential advisory relationship. People who earn commissions simply cannot be fiduciaries.

Other Professions

Tax preparers charge direct fees. You can do your own taxes and save money or you can delegate the task to a qualified professional. This professional will simplify your life, do a responsible job, and charge you a predictable fee for services rendered. In the future, consumers are simply going to have to decide whether they are going to act as their own advisor or pay for advice (and, if so, what a fair price might be).

Some professionals cost more than others in the same field, so the notion of identical pay for identical product placement regardless of advisor experience and sophistication will also change. In a transparent fee-based environment, everyone knows instinctively that it costs more to get a partner at a specialized Bay Street law firm to do legal work than it does to get a small-town generalist lawyer with a storefront office at the corner of Main and Elm to do the same work. It stands to reason that advisors with more experience and credentials and a higher profile and aptitude will command a higher fee than rookies will once fees become the prevailing compensation model for advisors. Some consumers who are currently on the fence and use an advisor only grudgingly might move to discount brokers. The advice channel doesn't want this, but the market segments itself pretty clearly. In general, either people want to work with an advisor or they don't, just as people choose whether or not to do their own tax preparation.

If qualified advice costs money, it logically follows

that it will cost more to work with an advisor than to do the work yourself. There are billions of dollars invested in mutual funds at discount brokerages, and they are paying these firms embedded fees even though no value-added services are being rendered. Annually, discount brokers earn tens of millions of dollars that rightfully belong in consumers' pockets. As it stands today, you can file your own tax return, hope you don't miss anything, and save yourself a few bucks in the process. You can defend yourself in court, take your chances with the judge and/or jury, and save yourself some legal fees. What you cannot do is invest by yourself using embedded-compensation funds without paying full (alleged) advisory fees.

Why Has Change Been So Slow?

So many advisors say they recommend embedded-compensation funds because only embedded-compensation funds pay them. There may be advisors who misrepresent details by telling clients they won't have to pay if they work together. Let's be clear here: *No funds pay advisors. Only consumers pay advisors.* The difference is that embedded-compensation funds have devised a seemingly benign way of collecting advisor compensation from clients and distributing it to advisors. One way or another, advisors are paid exclusively by their clients. It might also mean that advisors have to acknowledge that a good deal of their presumptive value proposition cannot be reliably substantiated.

As is often the case, change comes more quickly

where the competition is fiercest and the stakes are highest. Most of our major cities feature a wide range of STANDUP advisors offering their services to the public.

If most consumers are essentially indifferent, why should anyone, including regulators and legislators, care? This prevailing indifference may be largely due to consumers being blissfully unaware of how embedded compensation can cloud the judgment of advisors. *You can't be outraged by something you don't understand.*

On the client side of the equation, the most compelling reason to move to a fee-based arrangement is that it closely aligns client interests with advisor interests. Since fees are often based on the size of clients' portfolios, advisors have a clear incentive to make portfolios grow and to mitigate portfolio declines. The more the account grows, the more the advisor makes; the more the account declines, the less the advisor makes.

Compensation Logic

Do you know of any accountants who invoice themselves after preparing their own tax return? It would be a bit silly, wouldn't it? In fact, the concept is entrenched in law. For instance, you can hire a housecleaner or a gardener to do work around the house, but you can't legally pay yourself (or your spouse) for doing the same work.

Accountants bill their clients for services rendered, but there are millions of Canadians who file their own returns and forgo paying professional fees in the process. Whether it is wise to use a tax professional depends on the complexity of your situation and your ability to implement appropriate tax strategies. Nonetheless, it is a personal decision that people make on a household-by-household basis. However, no one in their right mind would bill themselves and then add the bill payment to their personal income. If an accountant were making $100,000 a year, would he bill himself an additional $700 to prepare his own return? He would have to give up about half that money in taxes—taxes that would otherwise not be due if he didn't bill himself.

Despite the ridiculousness of sending yourself a bill for services rendered, this is what many advisors do today. This is because most advisors buy mutual funds with embedded compensation for their own accounts. Even advisors who work at a conventional brokerage firm bill themselves for their own accounts. Does this sound like advisors might be compromised in some way? Would you entrust your life savings to someone who does this? What credibility do advisors have when they seem more interested in boosting their gross income through increased sales volume than in making sensible financial decisions *with their own money*?

Embedded-compensation mutual fund companies have made F-class mutual funds available to Canadians for over a decade now, and they insist that brokerage and planning firms have agreements and systems in place with all clients where F-class funds are purchased. The rationale is that they wouldn't want clients getting advice without paying for it. No advisor in their right mind would offer F-class funds to their clients without charging a separate fee because personal bankruptcy would surely follow. One can only do so much pro bono work.

The industry recognizes that it is unfair for advisors to have to bill themselves for doing their own financial planning (even though most advisors continue to do so) but does not recognize that an embedded fee for "advice" where no advice is given is unfair to consumers. If you're getting professional advice, you should expect to pay for it. It follows that if you're not getting advice, you shouldn't have to pay for it.

Embedded vs. Unbundled

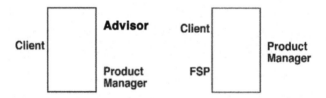

Whose side are you on? By moving to an unbundled format, advisors can demonstrate that they are aligning their practice with their clients' best interest. Without bunding, advisors are perceived as sales agents for the product manufacturers.

What Do Parts Cost?

Let's take a closer look at what product "parts" might cost. Depending on the arrangement with your advisor, you may have to pay to buy and sell investments, be they individual securities, mutual funds, exchange-traded funds (ETFs), or other products. In addition to trading costs, many products have ongoing annual costs (also known as management expense ratios, or MERs) associated with them. Individual securities have absolutely no cost associated with them. Most ETFs generally cost anywhere from 0.05% to 0.55%, and actively managed F-class mutual funds generally cost anywhere from 0.35% to 1.70%, so there's considerable room for variability depending on the products you use. In order to make a more meaningful disclosure to consumers, advisors could offer a listing of actual costs associated with each unbundled product. This way, consumers could see for themselves what the products cost and could simply add the advisor's fee on top. The total cost of the portfolio is simply the weighted average of the sum of the parts.

Many believe that the petroleum industry has done a good job of educating consumers about the constituent parts of their product costs. Big Oil has chosen to put pie charts on many of its pumps to demonstrate how they arrive at their price for gasoline. Of course, many believe this is because they want to point the finger at government taxes as a means of deflecting anger. Nonetheless, financial advisory firms could easily follow suit if they were genuinely committed to more and better disclosure.

Plenty of product recommendations are motivated at least somewhat by compensation issues. How is this monitored? At present, as long as the advisor can rationalize an investment as being consistent with client objectives, the investment choice goes largely unchallenged. The current test is one of product suitability. Practically speaking, however, it might be said that anything that isn't obviously unsuitable is likely suitable enough.

What Does Labour Cost?

Until the day when embedded compensation no longer exists, it should be noted that all advisors and their firms will soon have to make disclosures about the compensation they receive in each account. Transactional advisors naturally understand that they may well be forced to account for total charges more than before. Sales-oriented advisors depend on commissions. They will speak of the nobility and honour of earning commissions and of the many decent people who have done so for generations.

Advisor remuneration is tied to one of four factors: 1) direct fees on invested assets, 2) fees for services rendered, 3) commissions, and 4) salaries (which sometimes also involve bonuses). Let's take a look at each.

Direct Fees on Invested Assets

- No embedded compensation—the client pays fees directly and transparently
- Superior flexibility due to lack of restriction on future trading activity
- Calculated on the amount of assets in the client's portfolio

Fees, for example, might be 2% on all assets up to the first $125,000, 0.8% on additional assets up to $1,500,000, and 0.5% on all assets above that amount. Note how this sample schedule is scalable so that the percentage charged drops as the dollar amount goes up.

Amount Invested	Fee Percentage	Fee Dollar Amount
$125,000	2.00%	$2,500
$250,000	1.40%	$3,500
$500,000	1.10%	$5,500
$750,000	1.00%	$7,500
$1,000,000	0.95%	$9,500
$1,500,000	0.90%	$13,500
$2,000,000	0.80%	$16,000
$3,000,000	0.70%	$21,000
$6,000,000	0.60%	$36,000

Some might think of this as a volume discount. The 1% benchmark that many people seem to think is reasonable is reached at $750,000 invested. Accounts below this amount would cost more than 1% per year, and accounts above this amount would cost less. A fee-based format recognizes two important concepts: 1) the alignment of advisor and client interests, and 2) the economies of scale implicit in the rendering of advice. Since advisor compensation is linked to the size of the portfolio and not the placement of any product in particular, there is a clear consistency of purpose. If the account goes up, the advisor makes relatively more.

If the account drops, the advisor makes relatively less.

Many advisors make the point that they need more than 1% compensation for taking on smaller clients since these clients involve nearly as much work as larger ones. However, it simply isn't four times as much work to deal with one $1 million account as it is to work with four $250,000 accounts. Of course, the logic cuts both ways. If small accounts should command a premium, then large accounts should be accepted at a discount. The marginal fee rate format takes scalability into account.

Fees for Services Rendered (Not Related to Products at All)

- Usually only offered by "fee only" financial planners who often have no licence to sell investment products
- Written financial independence calculations (perhaps including a sensitivity analysis)
- Any projects involving reviewing, analyzing, and recommending specific objectives

With this option, the total fee depends on the time involved. For instance, the planner might charge $300 per hour, and the planner's assistant might charge $50 per hour.

Commissions

Some products such as life insurance and mutual funds pay a commission to the advisor's firm. As noted previously, this commission can be high up front with a smaller recurring trailing commission thereafter or it can be non-existent up front with a larger recurring trailing commission. In addition, many securities-licenced advisors (IIROC registrants) work using a transactional business model where they recommend the buying and selling of individual securities. They charge a commission for executing agreed-upon trades. The typical minimum charge for this sort of transaction is $85 to $125 per trade, and the amount charged often depends on the price of the security and the number of shares traded.

This used to be the dominant business model within the industry. Over the past decade or so, many advisors have moved voluntarily from this model to using direct fees. Fee-based revenues slightly exceed commission revenues at IIROC firms but still trail the revenues at both MFDA and insurance firms by a wide margin.

Salary

Many advisors work in bank branches for a set annual salary. These employees also often receive a bonus depending on various metrics that their employer might spell out as part of their employment contract. The good news about salaried advisors is that they are less likely to recommend something that is wholly unsuitable. They might be better equipped to help small investors look at the totality of their household balance sheet. For instance, traditional advisors might not get paid for getting a client to take out a mortgage, but a salaried advisor might very well have an incentive to do so. If a mortgage (i.e., taking on "good debt") is what is right for the client, this can be a very good thing.

However, bank advice is biased in a way, since bank advisors recommend only proprietary products and often work with clients who have more basic circumstances, but there's likely a reasonable matching of services and needs. The more obvious limitation is that if you work with someone at a bank, that person will only be able to sell you products from that institution. There's not necessarily anything wrong with that, but you should be aware from the outset that the "tools in the toolbox" will be relatively fewer with this sort of advisor.

Be Aware of Who You're Dealing With

The vast majority of advisors are decent people. This is true whether they are fee-based or commission-based. It is widely accepted that there is no meaningful correlation between advisor competence and the compensation model the advisor uses. Each model is generally thought to have many thorough and creative practitioners. As with any line of work, there are some who are better than others. It is vital to distinguish between competence and professionalism, which are very different things. Competence has to do with things such as qualifications and experience. Professionalism, on the other hand, is at least somewhat determined by the manner in which one works with clients.

From a client's perspective, working with an advisor is about getting high-quality, unbiased advice. For them, it all comes down to "Can I trust this person to recommend what is truly appropriate for my circumstances?" No matter how ethical, empathetic, competent, and professional an advisor seems to be, clients will instinctively wonder if their recommended products and strategies are what's best.

The GST of Financial Advice

The thing that keeps most people from working with a fee-based advisor is the fee itself. Many consumers who work with advisors who don't charge fees directly have probably never openly discussed the size of the bill. Putting advisor compensation out in the open changes that.

Perhaps the easiest way to understand the hatred many people feel about paying fees (especially in years when markets drop) is to consider how we reacted as a nation to the Goods and Services Tax (GST) when it was first introduced. Note that many provinces have since moved to a Harmonized Sales tax (HST). I was working on Parliament Hill in the summer of 1990, doing a work term for my graduate studies program in public administration. A special committee was set up to look into the effects of the GST on consumer prices. All manner of people and organizations came forward to express fear and loathing about the proposed changes to Canada's fiscal policy.

The members of the government of the day went to great lengths to explain that the tax would now be "transparent"—it would now be out in the open, whereas previously it had been embedded in the price of the final product. They insisted that the GST would replace an outdated tax system that charged large amounts for some things (manufactured goods) and nothing at all for others (services). Consumers weren't buying it. Putting a tax on sales receipts where none existed before created the distinct impression that taxes were going up, even though the GST proved to be essentially revenue neutral. This same phenomenon is a key issue when it comes to directly charging fees for financial advice.

Chapter 14
What Is Advice Really Worth?

Having looked at what products cost and the relative merits of product offerings at different price points, and having explored what qualified advice costs, we now come to what many feel is the crux of financial advice: What is it actually worth? To most commentators in the advice business, virtually all advice is worth far more than it costs. Of course, there are usually some pretty big exceptions. The obvious follow-up question is: If advice really is such a bargain, why has the industry not promoted the cost/benefit aspect of the bargain all of these years instead of embedding it to the point that many people think it is free? Indeed.

One such exception in the value story is often in relation to the value associated with robo-advisors. Most human advisors think robo-advisors represent poor value, even though they usually cost less than half of what human advisors cost. Is that so? In this chapter, we'll examine what evidence there is to see if we can get an accurate handle on the value of advice. The questions under consideration include the following:

- How can we realistically quantify the value of advice in general?
- What does the evidence say, and how reliable is the data overall?
- Are there circumstances where the general value might be higher or lower?
- If such circumstances exist, can we understand why and by how much the general value varies?

Please recognize that these sorts of questions do not lend themselves to scientific testing in a traditional sense. How does one reliably test the difference between what a client would have done and what they ended up doing as a result of an advisor's involvement? The outcomes are likely to vary wildly depending on each investor's individual tendencies. Let me disclose my own biases here:

- I very much favour good advice.
- I very much dislike bad advice.

Plenty of both kinds of advice exist out there, so distinguishing between them is critical.

To hear virtually all advisory firms, as well as many media commentators and product suppliers, tell it, almost all advisors are generally fantastic, value-adding professionals who act as personal coaches and lifestyle simplifiers for their valued clients. A smaller number of commentators have a more balanced view. I believe it is reasonable to expect that there will be both good and not-so-good practitioners in any line of work. I think it's about time that consumers had the tools to tell the difference in the financial services industry.

The list of purported value-adding services that advisors offer is both extensive and impressive. It includes the following:

- Tax optimization
- Setting and maintaining a suitable asset allocatio
- Regular account rebalancing
- Behavioural coaching
- Assistance in choosing between and integrating products and strategies
- Reminders about contribution and filing deadlines
- Assistance in understanding government programs
- Processing transactions
- Client education to help people better understand all of the above
- Various other services (this list is far from exhaustive)

Part of the difficulty in quantifying the value of advice is that it is hard to determine exactly what each of these things is worth. Another part is that some advisors do more things than others; the exact combination of services often varies considerably. I think most reasonable people would agree that different advisors have different approaches and that these, in turn, can affect (perhaps even dramatically) the value of the service offering. So far, the best we seem to be able to say about the subject is "it depends."

A few organizations have attempted to place a value on advice. As you might imagine, they usually take the items listed above and place some notional value on each of them…. X is worth 0.2% to 0.5%; Y is worth 0.1% to 0.3%; Z is worth 0.6% to 1.0%, etc. The general consensus from these organizations is that the value of financial advice is considerable but difficult to reliably quantify. One organization even went so far as to suggest that, all told, the value-added element of financial advice is about 3.0%.[32]

Other organizations use similar methods and arrive at different values—some higher, some lower. The services they often cite in addition to the main ones listed above include referrals, discipline, education, goal setting, estate planning, tax planning, portfolio tracking, and research. Even with these added, the list is still not exhaustive.

The research that uses the 3.0% number acknowledges that this quantification exercise "is not an exact science" and suggests that the value "will not appear on the quarterly statement but is real nonetheless."[33]

Some of the reasons put forward to justify these numbers are borderline comical. For instance, we can look at things from a "glass half full, glass half empty" perspective. One instance of so-called added value from one of the companies is that an advisor can add about 1% in expected return by substituting expensive products for cheaper ones—the glass is half full. What if we use the cheap products as the base case? Then using cheap products would add no value, and switching to expensive products would actually subtract 1% in value. The difference in cost is not in dispute. What's in dispute is the proper depiction of the value of advice depending on what the starting point of measurement is.

In this example, there might even be a third depiction. If the client would have bought an expensive product without an advisor but ended up buying a similarly expensive product when an advisor was involved, it might simply be a case of opportunity cost foregone, an opportunity to save money/add value that nonetheless was not taken, with no value added and none subtracted.

A second example is tax optimization. Lots of folks have been trained to think in terms of after-tax returns and therefore put their income investments in their tax-sheltered registered plans and their holdings that earn dividends and capital gains in their taxable accounts. For generations, this has been standard practice for enlightened investors. In the current environment, where bonds and GICs are paying next to nothing, it might actually make more sense to do the opposite. Even at the top tax bracket (more than 50% in most of Canada), the tax liability on a 1.5% return is just over 0.75%. Meanwhile, the tax on something earning even a modest 4.0% capital gain (using a 50% inclusion rate) would be just over 1.0%. In other words, depending on your assumptions (and actual experience) traditional tax optimization might do more harm than good. If this is true, is an advisor really adding value by encouraging clients to optimize their taxes this way?

A third example is what I have frequently referred to as "constructive behaviour modification" or "behavioural coaching," which generally means getting people to do things (or not do things) differently compared to what they would do if the advisor hadn't been involved. Think back to the chapter about behavioural finance. Most advisors know little, if anything, about behavioural finance. How, for instance, does an advisor get a client to recognize that they are refusing to sell out of a losing position because the client is anchored on the purchase price if the advisor doesn't even know what *anchoring* means? I'm not suggesting that an advisor who is familiar with the concept can't conceivably help, only that it is impossible to add value and fix a problem if you can't even recognize that there's problem in the first place.

Perhaps the most important consideration is how to fairly incorporate the one-by-one decision-making that goes on in most portfolio management. How do you measure what you did as a result of advice compared to what you might have done if you didn't get advice? Remember that over the course of a year, you might make a dozen or more decisions about your portfolio. How to disentangle the impact and value of each of those decisions to come to a meaningful depiction of the total impact of advice?

Given the examples above (there are others), it seems that most depictions of the value of advice are unreliable. It also stands to reason that the industry would want to portray itself in a favourable light.

What Does the Evidence Say?

There's a huge range in the things advisors do for their clients, the effectiveness of these things, and, by extension, the net value these things provide. For more than twenty years now, the people at the consulting firm DALBAR have released an annual report that compares actual investor returns to the returns earned by the mutual funds they invest in. Known as the "Quantitative Analysis of Investor Behavior" ("QAIB"), it is likely the most widely quoted research of its kind. While no similar studies exist for individual securities or ETFs, it is not too difficult to imagine where similarities might lie.

Here's a direct quote from the 2016 report:

Investment results are more dependent on investor behavior than on fund performance. Mutual fund investors who hold onto their investments have been more successful than those who try to time the market.[34]

Far from overcoming a well-documented "behaviour gap" by helping clients make smart decisions with their money, it seems advisors might actually be more likely to exacerbate the problem by chasing short-term performance. Of course, that is not necessarily true in a strict sense. This could also be a reverse beauty contest where advisors are just the least ugly option. In other words, advisors could be adding value by moderating (but not eliminating) self-destructive behaviour.

Instead of lagging fund performance by a moderate amount with an advisor, perhaps investors would have lagged by a massive amount if left to their own devices.

Remember that these numbers are aggregates. Actual experiences vary. Statisticians call this a wide dispersion. My sense is that the range of advice on offer today can lead to an extremely wide range of performance outcomes depending on several variables. If I were to hazard a guess, I'd say that outcomes are likely normally (evenly) distributed around the DALBAR numbers, with the best advisors coming in with modest positive numbers (i.e., they add some value) and the worst advisors coming in at shockingly negative ones (i.e., they subtract a lot).

A recent research report found that, in most cases, there was a strong correlation between how advisors invest and how their clients invest.[35] While both groups predictably invested in similar products and used similar strategies, the advisors' collective performance (4% below the benchmark) was worse than their clients' performance (3% below the benchmark)!

I need to stress that there's no truly reliable way to determine how much value a good advisor might add or how much a poor advisor might subtract when working with retail clients. The complaint about the industry at present is that many retail clients are overcharged, underserviced, and/or poorly advised. Most people have no real way of measuring those things when comparing one advisor to another. How do serious, client-centric advisors demonstrate their value? True differentiators must be the following:

- Legitimate: no hyperbole/overstatement of skill set
- High value: give people what they want/need
- Quantifiable: communicate and demonstrate value

I don't want you to get the wrong impression. People reading this might think I'm a financial advisor who is somehow self-loathingly anti-advisor. I am not in the least. I just don't buy the facile line that virtually all advice is good advice. Like many STANDUP advisors, I am adamant in my belief that good financial advice represents exceptional value to most retail investors and people in need of financial advice in general. The problem is that there are advisors out there who tend to cause considerable reputational risk for nearly all advisors. Consumers seem to have taken a "pox on all your houses" attitude.

Here are a few potential differentiators:

Good Advisors	Poor Advisors
• Manage and reduce costs and taxes	• Are indifferent to costs and taxes
• Don't believe past performance is reliable	• Often focus on past performance
• Maintain a strategic asset allocation	• Often have no formal strategy at all
• Encourage "buy low, sell high" behaviour	• Enable emotional, media-driven behaviour
• Are interested in clients' lives and problems	• Are interested in market moves and forecasts
• Communicate consistently and often	• Seldom communicate
• Generally do not try to time markets	• Frequently try to time markets

Testing for a reaction is perhaps the surest way to determine your advisor's value and utility. People who are good at what they do are generally not going to be threatened by new entrants, obligations, disclosures, or business models. Those who are not so good, however, tend to react defensively. In a world where clients will, for the first time, know exactly how much they're paying for financial advice, the financial services industry may very well segment itself. The good advisors will likely invite and encourage value-for-money discussions, while the poor advisors may try to change the subject.

Less Is More

Depending on how you keep score, there are likely more financial advisors in Canada than there are doctors. Since everyone should have access to medical advice and not everyone needs financial advice, the advice business might simply have too many people in it right now. For instance, no one under eighteen can have an investment account, and there are millions of Canadians who have no appreciable investment assets (let's say they have less than $25,000).

If among 36 million Canadians 8 million are under eighteen and a further 8 million have less than $25,000 to invest, then the number of people who actually need an advisor would be just over half the number of people who need a doctor. Except for the matter where you might only see a doctor for a 10-minute meeting, while a meeting with a financial advisor could take hours, it seems intuitively plausible that we could get by with far fewer advisors than we have. Virtually every advisor I know is eagerly accepting new clients. Meanwhile, newspapers now run stories about people having difficulty accessing medical advice.

David Thompson, a senior executive at AXA Wealth, recently pointed out that there is one advisor for every 2,900 people in the UK compared to one for every 1,400 people in the US and one for every 1,900 people in Canada.[36] It seems as though a few advisors could certainly be trimmed. As a simple hypothetical illustration, let's say there are 100,000 advisors in Canada working with 200 families each on average (20 million Canadians with an advisor in total). Suppose the industry were to cull a third of all advisors. We'd be left with just under 67,000 advisors working with about 300 families each on average.

There are people who would have you believe that the previous passage is financial services heresy. There are likely very few STANDUP advisors in that group, however. The primary concern here needs to be the welfare of the general public, not the overall population of financial advisors.

Disruption Is Coming

There are many examples of the creative destruction caused by technological disruptions. Technology has changed the way we build cars, drive cars, and hail cabs. It has changed the way we travel and the way we find places to travel to. In fact, technology has changed virtually every industry in one way or another. It would be folly to think even for a moment that the financial services industry is immune to such change. If anything, the industry is a prime candidate for technological disruption. It has already happened once. A generation ago, automatic teller machines (ATMs) put a small army of bank tellers out of work. Today, so-called robo-advisors may well end up doing something similar.

Over the past year and a half, a growing number of robo-advisor firms have sprung up in Canada and around the world. Robo-advisors are simply technology-enabled online offerings that assist retail clients with basic investment advice and execution. They occupy a position somewhere between discount brokerages (for DIY investors) and full-service advisors (for people who need more advice and/or prefer a human advisor). Robo-advisor services generally cost more than those offered by discount brokerages and less than those offered by human advisors. While occupying a middle ground on pricing, robo-advisors also offer a middle ground in terms of advice and service. There's a new way to segment the "you get what you pay for" continuum.

Does a mid-tier service offering at a mid-tier price represent a compelling proposition? Since robo-advisors are so new, no one can offer a reliable answer at this point. As with the questions of competency and transparency, the best advisors, and even average advisors, have no reason to feel threatened by something as novel as an upstart robo-advisor offering or three. The advisors who occupy the lowest tiers are the ones who should be worried. Advisors with client bases consisting mainly of clients with less than $100,000 invested in simple RRSPs, TFSAs, and RESPs will likely soon need to either sharpen their pencils or update their resumes. In short, they are at the risk of losing clients who take a serious look at robo-advisor offerings. If nothing else, a robo-advisor offering is almost certainly at least 1.0% cheaper than their current service offering.

One thing I enjoy when I hear human advisors offering input on robo-advisors are their doubts about how well robo-advisors will fare in the event of an inevitable market downturn. Their logic is that many people would not have the confidence and emotional fortitude to stay the course with robo-advisors if markets began to plunge. Although the evidence is flimsy, markets in Canada dropped quickly in the first six weeks of 2016, and virtually all robo-advisors reported no material change in client behaviour.

This doesn't prove much. In fact, there's too little evidence to say anything with certainty at this point. The thing about robo-advisors, however, is that most of the people using them today are millennials, who are in their mid twenties to mid thirties and who have the natural benefits of a very long time horizon but relatively little money invested.

The human advisors who are eager to see how robo-advisors fare in a down market might need to be careful about what they wish for. The larger, older, and sometimes less sophisticated clients that they currently work with strike me as being far more likely to do something rash than a typical client of robo-advisors. What if the evidence ultimately shows that robo-advisors do better at behavioural coaching and constructive behaviour modification than human advisors? I'm not saying that it'll play out one way or another, only that people who presume they'll defeat a machine had better be careful. In the mid 1990s, Deep Blue, a computer developed by IBM, beat chess grandmaster and World Chess Champion Gary Kasparov. Now IBM is developing Watson, a computer system capable of natural language processing and machine learning. In 2011, Watson competed on the trivia game show *Jeopardy!* against two of the biggest former winners in the show's history, and the computer won the first place prize of $1 million. In short, computer systems are getting extremely sophisticated over a relatively short period. Is it really such a stretch that computers with a 1.0%+ cost advantage should be able to beat financial advisors in a situation where emotions are a very real factor?

Another important point about the value of advice is that it is possible that more people will choose to become DIY investors down the road. Many people are currently of the mistaken opinion that financial advice is free. Others know that there's a cost involved but cannot quantify what that cost might actually be. It stands to reason that some people in both groups will, once they come to understand just how much qualified advice actually costs, choose to forego that advice and act as their own financial advisor. I'm not saying that choice is either right or wrong, only that it seems a likely outcome for some people. We're just getting to the point where clients understand price. Accordingly, we're also just getting to the point where clients can finally assess value. It has been said that price is an issue only in the absence of value. One could just as easily say that people can focus on value only when they understand price.

Recently published papers show that financial advisors do indeed improve financial outcomes for investors provided that the interests of the advisors and the interests of the investing household are aligned. These same papers also show that professional advice can cause harm if conflicts of interest create high agency costs.[37] In other words, they say that embedded compensation has been shown to reduce the quality of advice.

The irony in all of this is that proponents of embedded compensation have long been insisting that banning that option would make financial advice less affordable. Here's a direct quote from Greg Pollock, the president and CEO of Advocis: "If a ban on commissions is successful, as some are calling for, we [could] see a sharp decline in access to professional advice because those who need it most won't be able to afford it."[38] As mentioned previously, charging the same amount but in a different way has absolutely no impact on affordability whatsoever. For instance, clients could pay by having quarterly redemptions done in their accounts. The amount they pay for advice would be the same, and it would come from the same place.

The only difference is that they would now see a line item on their statement. The ultimate amount deducted (i.e., the affordability) would likely not be affected. Given all the drawbacks, my view is that society cannot afford to keep embedded compensation. With the price of advisory services out in the open, consumers will finally be able to judge for themselves whether or not they're getting value for their money.

Here's where it gets really interesting. In the final section of the book, we'll take a look at what may happen—not because some advisors want to do it but because all advisors may be forced to change due to legislated reforms. Until about now, STANDUP advisors have been doing what is right voluntarily while hoping to get clients who understand and appreciate their taking an evidence-based approach. In the near future, it seems likely that all advisors may need to display these attributes because the law will demand it.

PART 4

PROFESSIONALISM

CHAPTER 15
REGULATORY ARBITRAGE

It is time to put all the pieces together. In Part 1, we laid out how advisors are trained, licensed, and regulated. In Part 2, we talked about evidence and the need to be aware of it so that advisors can give advice based on the most current and accurate information available. In Part 3, we talked about disclosure and ultimately disintermediation. How much do financial products and financial advice cost, and how can we be sure that consumers are making informed decisions about what they're paying for?

Part 4 deals with professionalism, something that brings all of these elements together in a total package. The first three sections dealt with how the best advisors can win the day by being more transparent, professional, and client-centred by focusing on those attributes voluntarily. A sizable minority of advisors has already begun to take several of the trappings of STANDUP advice on their own. Part 4 deals with things that regulators and legislators are enacting to make STANDUP advice unavoidable. In Chapter 1, I stated that I had a dream where all advisors would consistently and predictably do what is right for their clients. This is how the dream ends.

Another way of looking at this is to say that the ideas discussed in Parts 1 through 3 are the sorts of things that decent, progressive, client-centred advisors can do right now if they want to. It should be obvious that there are nonetheless some advisors who will resist change until they must comply with new laws that enforce a STANDUP approach. More precisely, Part 4 is about what other jurisdictions have already done elsewhere and what is under way here in Canada to force advisors to be more transparent, cost-sensitive, and evidence-based so that all consumers can feel assured that they're receiving proper advice.

As you now know, there are three primary areas where an advisor can be licensed in Canada: insurance, mutual funds, and securities. Before 1987, these three industries were essentially treated as "silos." Of course, over the past thirty years or so, the financial services industry has moved toward a one-stop shopping sort of experience where a single trusted advisor can (ideally) provide whatever product or service you need.

Even though the industry is talking a good game about being comprehensive and holistic in the services it offers, the reality is that old habits die hard, and pre-existing regulators are not exactly eager to give up their jurisdiction. In other words, the three product silos have three different regulators—each with their own rules and standards. For any given advisor, the prevailing rules depend on the prevailing product, and if the advisor is licensed to sell more than one product type, there will be different standards of disclosure and competency depending on the product the advisor recommends.

Regulatory Arbitrage

Speaking in extremely broad brush strokes, the highest standards apply to securities, followed by mutual funds and then insurance. Since many advisors are (or could easily be) licensed for multiple product types, there's a fairly obvious opportunity for advisors who actively resist transparency and avoid making evidence-based recommendations to use products that have the lowest regulatory standards. In layman's terms, this can lead to a race to the bottom, where advisors who resist the STANDUP paradigm begin to slide over to the products and services provided through the regulator with the lowest standards. This phenomenon is sometimes referred to as "regulatory arbitrage."

As a practical matter, advisors who are licensed to sell securities are held to the regulatory standards of securities when recommending mutual funds. Accordingly, the problem that many believe could present itself in the short term is that some securities and mutual fund registrants will avoid making more meaningful disclosures to clients by instead selling the insurance-industry equivalent of mutual funds, something known as segregated funds.

Segregated funds are similar to mutual fund investments but have a built-in insurance contract.

Policyholders are given a guarantee on a portion of their principal investment while at the same time are able to invest their money in an investment portfolio made up of what amounts to underlying mutual funds. In contrast to traditional mutual funds, segregated funds do not require the presale disclosure of major product details. In short, there is no segregated fund equivalent to the fund facts documents that mutual fund purchasers are required to receive before making a purchase. Due to the insurance contract element, segregated fund management-expense ratios (MERs) can be 0.5% to 1.5% higher than the cost of a mutual fund.

The securities and mutual fund industries are set to begin reporting on both total compensation (to both the advisors and their firms) and performance in January 2017. There are no corresponding reporting obligations regarding insurance products. This is likely the clearest evidence that the retail advice system should not be driving the regulations that control it. For perhaps the first time in history, it now looks like segregated fund asset levels are growing more quickly than mutual fund asset levels.

Regulation by Product

Regulation by product is a big part of the problem, in my opinion. We need to put down a single, consistent, and enforceable standard across the country irrespective of province of residence or product licensing. As it stands, Canada's patchwork systems (both by political jurisdiction and by product line) combine to slow the pace of reform while ordinary investors—seniors in particular—are at risk. Older people simply don't understand the paperwork and current disclosures being made. Furthermore, it is entirely possible that they'll never know enough to be able to make meaningful, informed choices.

To deal with the problem, perhaps we could take our cues from regulators in other jurisdictions. For instance, Hong Kong implemented its version of a fund facts document for all financial products within eighteen months. Canada's reforms have taken over a decade, and we're still not done.

For those who suggest that better enforcement of the rules is the issue, I beg to differ. There's no real value in putting more enforcement behind inadequate rules. Better rules and higher standards need to come first. As such, the recent changes in Canada still do not go to the core of dealing with conflicts of interest and advisor bias. For instance, does anyone else find it interesting that segregated funds, which are often criticized because of their relatively high fees, are seeing newfound popularity just as fees in the wealth management business are increasingly coming under the microscope? Furthermore, recently enacted regulatory changes do not require financial advisors to include increased disclosures on fees or product performance on segregated funds. The same holds true for bank products such as index-linked notes, principal-protected notes, and guaranteed investment certificates.

The great irony in all of this is that the financial services industry is effectively creating and exacerbating a problem. According to Susan Eng, a former executive director of CARP (formerly known as the Canadian Association of Retired Persons), many older Canadians are (effectively?) avoiding the industry entirely. This, in turn, magnifies—and possibly even creates—a savings crisis. Not surprisingly, most entrenched players in the industry look at our dismal savings rates and allege that the solution lies in having more advisors, who would presumably help ordinary people save more. These same product manufacturers also opposed the recent expansion of the Canada Pension Plan (CPP) on the grounds that it will act as a disincentive for personal savings. Some went so far as to suggest that the expansion of the CPP is a de facto employer payroll tax. Whenever I hear this line of reasoning, I ask these people if they think the CPP should be abolished. To date, no one has ever suggested such a thing.

Rather than simply lament what has not happened in Canada, let's turn our attention to international developments, including a few positive developments here in our own backyard.

CHAPTER 16
THE GLOBAL MARCH TO A STANDUP MODEL

Progress almost never proceeds in an uninterrupted straight line. Instead, it tends to proceed in fits and starts where long periods of modest change are punctuated by spasms of reform. When the first edition of this book was released in 2003, the idea of STANDUP advice gaining acceptance bordered on heresy. Times have changed.

In the US, passive strategies have brought in US$229 billion in net new assets in the first half of 2016. Over the same period, active strategies have lost US$236 billion in net assets.[39] People are making informed decisions out of self-interest even before regulators require advisors to do what might be right for clients. We can debate about whether advisors or clients are leading this trend, but either way, there is no doubt that cost-effective, transparent products are quickly coming to rule the roost.

Despite this trend, many advisors have come to the conclusion that they would rather hire "expert professionals" (i.e., money managers) to run specific mandates within their clients' portfolios. Whether advisors are trading securities themselves or subcontracting it to specialists, the proposition remains. Here's what Chet Currier, a columnist at Bloomberg, had to say about it:

> What mutual funds have always had to sell is diversification, convenience, liquidity, and something called "professional management." Well, the customers can get all the diversification, convenience, and liquidity they want from index funds that avoid the costs of security selection.... Active managers deserve to be paid only for the amount by which they outperform the index, known by the shorthand term *alpha*. Because active managers as a group stand little chance of beating the market (they are the market and they cannot hope to beat themselves), those active managers as a group deserve no pay at all.[40]

But if traditional active managers do such a collectively poor job on the performance side that they don't deserve any pay at all, why would any professional, independent, client-centred advisor ever recommend using their services? It appears that there is an undemonstrated presumption of value at play. Even though there is some evidence that beating the market is sometimes possible, there is no reliable evidence that it can be done predictably, reliably, or persistently.

Lots of People "Get It"

There are those who would have us believe that matters of high finance are too difficult to grasp for ordinary people who are not financial experts. My view is that it's actually far more basic than that. Throughout history, people from various walks of life have offered pearls of wisdom that we can apply to the challenges we're grappling with here. They didn't weigh in on financial challenges such as advisor bias, the proper alignment of interests, or competing value propositions, but they did offer some timeless and universal perspectives on human nature in general. Many of their comments show that they "get it" regarding the challenges we face today.

German philosopher Arthur Schopenhauer is said to have mused, "All truth passes through three stages. First, it is ridiculed. Second, it is violently opposed. Third, it is accepted as being self-evident." Today, the idea of giving financial advice based on verifiable evidence is violently opposed. Can the ultimate acceptance of such a self-evidently sensible approach be far behind?

American composer John Cage once said, "I can't understand why people are frightened of new ideas. I'm frightened by the old ones." The resistance to change, no matter how purposeful and client-centred, seems alive and well in the modern financial services industry.

Norwegian playwright Henrik Ibsen once wrote, "I hold that man is in the right who is most closely in league with the future." The future may be closer than we think. Many of the concepts discussed so far have already been enacted into law in big developed countries around the English-speaking world. While the jury is still largely out regarding what it all means, there is no doubt that it's all happening.

International Developments

In 2009, the regulatory authority in the UK at the time, the Financial Services Authority (FSA), issued rules that codified and established a fee model for advisors in the UK. These rules took effect in January 2012.

As a jurisdiction that had been using what is known as a principles-based regulatory regime, the UK decided it would be desirable to establish new, clear-cut standards that would effectively raise the bar for advisors. Sound familiar? Their intent was to remove the incentive trade-off between commissions and suitability in the hope that it would increase the suitability of products being sold to investors. The new rules required advisors to set their own fees. As such, in the UK, there is now a requirement to disclose the cost of advice and the cost of investment products separately. In addition, the UK regulator raised the minimum qualification level for advisors, instituted a code of ethics, and boosted requirements for continuing education.

The comment letters that the FSA received before enacting the reforms were particularly telling. Some stakeholders warned that many advisors would be forced to leave the business if the reforms that were ultimately enacted came to pass. Similar warnings are being made in Canada. Not only is it unclear that this would happen, it is unclear that it would be a bad thing if it did!

The UK is not alone. In April 2010, the Australian government, under Prime Minister Kevin Rudd, announced reforms with similar objectives. In a press release announcing the initiative, the minister responsible, Chris Bowen, said, "These reforms will see Australian investors receive financial advice that is in their best interests, rather than being directed to products as a result of incentives or commissions offered to the financial advisor."[41]

Australia's Future of Financial Advice (FOFA) package included:

* A prospective ban on conflicted remuneration structures
* The introduction of a statutory fiduciary duty
* Increased transparency and flexibility of payments, including advisor charging
* Percentage-based fees charged only on unbundled products with investor consent
* The expanded availability of low-cost, simple advice

The majority of these reforms came into effect in 2012. In the first half of 2012, Australian advisors transitioned in earnest in order to be prepared for the new reality that awaited them. One part of the new Australian practices is the concept of a centralized investment proposition (CIP). When making investment recommendations to clients, Australian advisors are now required to disclose all expenses and fees associated with not only the products they recommend but also the alternatives they do not recommended. The onus is now on the advisor to demonstrate why they believe the client will be better off as a result of their preferred course of action.

Shortly after embedded compensation was banned in both Australia and the UK, there was a clear shift away from higher-cost products to lower-cost products. In fact, according to Nick Blake, the head of retail distribution for Vanguard Asset Management Ltd. in the UK, the UK reforms have led to greater emphasis on product suitability for clients thanks to a fee-based structure, enhanced professional standards, and greater clarity on advisor status.[42]

New Evidence of Disclosure Failure

For years, the thinking in many circles (and here I freely confess that I was part of the problem) was that things would be much better if we only had more and better disclosure. People who wanted to make things better advocated for disclosure because it was perceived to work. Apparently, that's not the case.

Sunita Sah, a professor at Georgetown University, has done some research where she showed that disclosure does not work in mitigating conflicts of interest. In fact, it often backfires. She showed that consumers often ignore or discount caveats disclosed at the beginning of an advisory relationship, and many actually feel compelled to comply with recommendations precisely because the disclosures were made at the outset. Talk about unintended (sometimes called "perverse") consequences! Her research showed that disclosure regarding conflicts of interest on the part of an advisor is often perceived as being tantamount to a request for a favour.

Astonishingly, the research found that clients were *more inclined to take conflicted advice* after advisors had made disclosures, with no exceptions regardless of gender or age. A not-too-surprising consequence is that it also found that advisors gave more conflicted advice if it was accompanied with disclosure. As it happens, the opposite is true in the field of medicine. In all cases, the financial advice turned out to be less biased if advisors were reminded of their duty of care to clients beforehand. It seems that disclosure works best when it changes advisor behaviour. Not surprisingly, other jurisdictions have made the transition from disclosure to disintermediation, perhaps because they feared the sorts of adverse consequences that Sah has discovered.

Disclosure seems to be a particularly poor means of dealing with information asymmetries because most small retail investors are at a massive disadvantage relative to their advisors in terms of what they know, what they can reasonably call upon to learn more, and what they can do to gain some degree of pricing power. The objective of regulatory reform is to arrive at better outcomes. If disclosure alone fails to do that, then it stands to reason that disclosure alone is not enough. It seems that the reforms we need are wider-ranging than we first thought. If disclosure cannot manage conflicts, it may well be that we need to take steps to eliminate those conflicts altogether.

People all over the world are watching the evolving developments and changes abroad. What happens elsewhere will likely be similar to what we're set to experience here in Canada. No one doubts that there will be some amount of confusion, dislocation, and trouble, but the early results are promising. Purposeful reforms (provided that they really are purposeful) have positive effects. Incidentally, the regulators in the UK also say that they have not seen any evidence of an advice gap in the supply of professional advice.

What's Been Going on in Canada?

Well over a decade ago, Ontario proposed some regulatory changes, championing an approach that was controversially named the Fair Dealing Model (FDM). After going as far as the province could, Ontario passed the proposals on to the Canadian Securities Administrators (CSA) in the hope of taking enhanced regulatory oversight on matters such as suitability, reporting, and transparency to the national stage. The CSA, the combined provincial and territorial regulators from across the country, were to be the new custodians in charge of regulatory reform. Their intent was presumably to standardize many of the original Ontario Securities Commission (OSC) ideas and make them applicable across the country. Politics and regulation being what they are, the price of wide-ranging interprovincial agreement seems to be perpetual compromise and delay. The good news is that we have made progress. The bad news is that the progress has been both modest and painfully slow in coming. What emerged from years of horse-trading was something called the Client Relationship Model (CRM) (sometimes called CRM1), which has already been implemented. The adoption of the CRM on March 26, 2012, finally spelled out advisors' requirements regarding relationship disclosures and conflict management.

Our regulators have elected to require that the client and advisor have a discussion about what services the advisor will provide and how the client will pay for them when they open the account. For existing clients, there was a transition period that allowed advisors to give clients similar disclosures. Conflict of interest is something that advisors and their firms are now required to avoid if at all possible, and to disclose and control at any rate. Many people (myself included) doubt that advisors can practically manage conflicts of interest and biases through disclosure. Our view is that we should eliminate all such conflicts.

To repeat, avoiding and addressing conflicts, including the perception of conflicts, must now be spelled out in writing before opening new accounts. Advisors are required to issue these same disclosures on existing accounts before completing trades. It is self-evident that advisors and their firms are in implicit conflict with clients given that they want to make money off their clients, and the more they charge, the less the clients get to keep. Still, the adoption of CRM was the first time that even such basic conflicts were acknowledged in writing.

The bar has clearly moved in determining client account suitability. Until the spring of 2012, the factors advisors considered when assessing the suitability of a particular product or security for a client included current financial situation, investment knowledge, investment objectives, risk tolerance, and any other factors that we might deem noteworthy. Once CRM came into effect, advisors added new considerations, including liquidity, time horizon, relationship disclosure, conflict of interest management and disclosure, suitability assessment, and investing for a specific use.

Advisors are now expected to consider the client's time horizon and the portfolio's overall compositional risk level in doing suitability assessments. I was rather surprised to learn that those factors were not considered a part of the original suitability review process. Six months after the original CRM adoption (September 26, 2012), the revised rule regarding suitability assessment came into force. That's when the new test of "trigger events" regarding suitability standards kicked in. Until that date, updates occurred only when there was a material change to a client's circumstances (e.g., divorce, new job, birth of a child, new residence) or when a trade was inconsistent with a client's profile. Before that date, compliance departments were required to do a suitability review only when trading activity seemed inconsistent with client objectives. As of that date, accounts are to be managed while bearing in mind certain trigger events that might transpire. For instance, the Canadian stock market dropped by about 20% between its 2015 high and the beginning of 2016. If such a drop caused a client's asset allocation to deviate materially from what the client and the advisor deemed suitable when they opened the account, a review would be in order.

Issuers could face trigger events, too. For instance, a security (or a number of securities) could be transferred in kind from another institution. That transfer might cause a portfolio's characteristics to deviate materially from the initial suitability assessment. A review would be in order in this case as well.

Yet another example would be if a client changed advisors within the same firm. They originally slated performance reporting as a fourth major reform to implement via the CRM, but they ultimately postponed it to the next round of reform.

CRM2

On July 15, 2016, the most recent round of regulatory reform in Canada came into effect. This being Canada, one of arguably only two industrialized countries on earth without a national securities regulator, the earlier Ontario initiative continued to be compromised repeatedly in an effort to gain a national consensus via the Canadian Securities Administrators (CSA). The CSA is simply the sum of all provincial and territorial securities commissions. In the case of CRM2, the outcome is not so much an example of too many cooks spoiling the broth as it is of too many cooks adding too much water to the offering over the course of a decade.

I'll take an optimistic perspective and acknowledge that oftentimes something is better than nothing, even if so much more could have been done. In fairness, I should also note that there are those who feel that the initial reforms, while laudable in intent, were impractical as far as implementation was concerned.

As of January 2017, advisors are to disclose certain new information to clients on their statements. Monthly statements are expected to remain much the same until then. Some people will see the new format of statements earlier. For most people, the first actual statements that will record the "annual report of charges and other compensation" and "annual report on investment performance" will be sent out in the beginning of 2017 and will reflect information as it was on December 31, 2016. In other words, in the coming months, it is hoped that investors will see in simple terms exactly how much they are paying their advisor's firm (the advisor receives only a portion of this money) and how well their portfolio has been performing over the last little while.

This information will be old news for some people. Investors working with fee-based advisors already get an annual statement verifying total fees paid, and those working with portfolio managers (i.e., those using discretionary accounts) also get quarterly performance reports. But even for them, standardized reporting will be modified. For most people, however, this will be totally new. The big question is, what will change, really?

It seems that everyone has an opinion. To be sure, more transparency and accountability is a step in the right direction. Just how big a step are we talking about? In my opinion, the improved disclosure of performance will likely be more effective than the improved disclosure of the cost of advice. Ironically, most people are expecting a fallout regarding the disclosure of advisor compensation. Perhaps the real trouble will arise when people connect dots when it comes to questionable value coupled with considerable cost.

Various studies have shown that a large percentage of people are still under the misguided impression that financial advice is free. Even among those who know that they're paying for advice, there are some who cannot adequately explain how or how much they're paying their advisor. While the amount paid varies from advisor to advisor, the primary variables are the advisor's business model, the client's asset allocation, and the client's account size (usually measured on a household basis).

One thing that some people might not have thought of is that there may have been at least a few DSC (deferred sales charge) mutual fund purchases deliberately made in late 2015. In a hypothetical scenario like that, DSC purchases would generate an upfront payment to the advisor the week that the purchase was made. With such purchases made in 2015, the upfront amount would not be reported as a part of the payments made to the advisor in 2016. For the advisors who did this, there are three potential benefits:

1. Getting a payday in 2015 without registering any related payments in 2016
2. Having a lower stated income in 2016 relative to placing money into front-end versions (trailers on DSC equity funds are typically 0.5%, whereas trailers on front-end funds are typically 1.0%)
3. Having the client who bought the DSC fund locked in for a further seven years or so for funds purchased on a DSC basis

In short, even as the industry moves toward greater transparency, there are will always be opportunities to skirt intentions. Note that there is nothing illegal about this tactic.

My guess is that there will be a modest to moderate amount of shock and dislocation as a result of the statements going out in early 2017. What remains to be seen is just how violently investors will react when they see how much their advisors are paid. My sense is that the degree of outrage should correspond to the gravity of the problem. To me, this means that if most people take the information in stride, then perhaps the problem is not as bad as some are making it out to be. Most investors should expect somewhere just above 1% of total assets invested. Investors with smaller accounts might be surprised to see that they're paying more. While the numbers may vary, here's my guess of what most people will see:

Account Size	Compensation Range As a Percentage	Compensation Range in Dollars
$100,000	1.2% to 2.0%	$1,200 to $2,000
$200,000	1.1% to 1.6%	$2,200 to $3,200
$500,000	1.0% to 1.3%	$5,000 to $6,500
$1,000,000	0.9% to 1.1%	$9,000 to $11,000

For those who thought that their advisor was working for free (i.e., that their advisor was working as an act of charity), this will be a rude awakening. There may be some anger, but I believe that cooler heads will ultimately prevail and people will get over it.

To my mind, the bigger issue will likely be performance. In the post-global-financial-crisis world of 2016, there are still far too many "I brake for unicorns" type investors out there. Polls and studies delving into investor expectations show that many people are living in a fantasyland. The Financial Planning Standards Council (FPSC) recently released their long-term planning projection assumptions for Certified Financial Planners (CFPs). Those numbers are modest but realistic—unlike most investors. Many studies and polls have shown that most investors—and millennials in particular—have unrealistically high expectations about future returns. I would go so far as to say that most boomer investors and retired investors face similar concerns and that most advisors do too little to disabuse them of these notions, especially the advisors who don't really take costs into account.

As noted in Part 1 of the book, the FPSC recommends that planners aim for about a 5.0% return on a balanced portfolio *before fees and costs are applied*. Assuming a 2.0% inflation rate, that's a total real return of only 3.0% above inflation *before fees and costs are applied*. If total product costs and advisory fees come to 2.0%, then the total return after costs and after inflation would be a paltry 1.0%. Now do you see why cost is so vitally important?

This brings us to another point. So far, we've only been talking about what CRM2 does. We haven't discussed what it *doesn't* do. You may be surprised to learn that there is absolutely no mention of product costs in the new CRM2 disclosures. Remember, product cost is different from advisor compensation, and only the latter will be disclosed under CRM2 reforms. Although they have previously implemented cost-related rules and regulations, including point-of-sale disclosure and a statutory pre-purchase requirement for both the mutual fund facts and ETF facts documents, the concern that I have is that uneven cost reporting will effectively have the unintended consequence of misleading investors. Why disclose one (the cost of products) at the point of sale and another (the cost of advice) on client statements? Product cost disclosure is covered separately in point-of-sale disclosures via fund facts documents.

Imagine getting your car repaired and having the

mechanic give you a bill for the labour while requesting a blank cheque for the parts. As it stands, advisors will soon tell investors how much they are paying for labour (financial advice), but disclosures about how much the parts (mutual funds, ETFs, etc.) cost will not appear on the confirming invoice statement, although they disclose those details before you buy. How's that for encouraging meaningful price shopping?

Many people, myself included, had high hopes for what improved disclosure might mean for the public. What has emerged thus far is a more convoluted disclosure approach. The good news is that positive change is coming. In my view, however, we're more than a decade behind where we could (and should) be if meaningful, client-centred reforms had been implemented when they were needed.

Possible Ban on Embedded Compensation

Armed with the Cumming report and Brondesbury report findings (see Chapter 12), the CSA is aiming to release a discussion paper by the end of 2016 about how to go about banning embedded compensation. This is a sensitive topic, and it is important to recognize that not all jurisdictions see eye to eye. Still, now that empirical data has confirmed intuitions about causation, the path toward purposeful action seems to be opening up.

Once they release their paper, the CSA plans on holding in-person consultations in early 2017 to further explore the option of banning embedded compensation, presumably on an operational level of "How do we best go about doing this?" It will take some time for them to consider the feedback they receive. This feedback will come through both written and in-person consultations, so it may well be mid 2017 before the CSA is ready to announce whether it will be moving ahead with an actual rule proposal.

There are political considerations within the CSA that complicate and extend the process. Much as I lament the glacial pace of change, I should note that I applaud our regulators' objective of making only evidence-based policy decisions. They want to ensure that they give all market participants a thorough opportunity to provide compelling fact-based evidence on why banning would or would not yield the right outcomes for investors in Canada. In particular, the primary aim of their consultations will be to compel the industry to move past simplistic responses and to explain how banning embedded compensation might specifically affect our market, given what we know about our fund managers, dealers, and investors. The CSA's paper will lay out compelling Canadian data in that regard. It will also lay out an analysis of other anticipated effects of a ban on commissions on the mutual fund industry in Canada. It will be up to the industry to demonstrate where regulators are wrong and to bring attention to any potential unintended consequences that regulators may have overlooked. Everyone will need to support all of this with evidence rather than simply make abstract comparisons to the experiences of other jurisdictions.

What Canadian Regulators Could Do

Having looked at what others have done internationally and what we have either enacted or at least slated to discuss in Canada, let's turn our attention to what's a little further down the road. There are many ideas either regulatory in nature (fiduciary status) or legislative in nature (regulating advisors in general and financial planners in particular) that remain farther along the horizon. It should be noted that the IIROC, the investment industry's primary self-regulatory organization, has always insisted that the bar is already set appropriately for matters of disclosure, competency, and investor protection. Perhaps we should revisit and ultimately redefine the question of requisite disclosure of material facts.

The financial services industry depends on maintaining the trust of the people who hope that the industry is transparent and ethical enough to conduct itself in a matter deserving of that ongoing trust. In my view, many of the industry's non-disclosures materially affect choices and outcomes. Moving to a STANDUP model could very well cause investors to make different decisions if these disclosures were made. A significant part of the problem surrounding the glacial pace of reform is that regulators only react to perceived problems when a large number of people complain or when there are scandals that compel them to protect those that are most vulnerable. Mercifully, we have had relatively few of those in Canada, especially on the part of advisors.

A decade or so ago, there was a medium-sized

problem where many mutual fund companies allowed hedge funds and institutional investors to buy their products overnight while securities were being traded on the other side of the globe. This amounted to allowing certain investors to, for instance, buy when it was obvious that the market they were buying into was heading up and sell when it was obvious that the fund they were selling would open lower the next day. Regulators slapped the funds in question with a few fines, and that was the end of it. The firms in question noted that there was nothing illegal with this conduct.

Some take the position that the system is working fine simply because there haven't been many major scandals to date. To my mind, the operative words are *to date*. Most people buy property insurance for their homes even though they hope to never need it. Floods, fires, and the like are not the sort of thing one would ordinarily expect. People expect the best but prepare for the worst. So it should be with industry regulation. Just because your house hasn't burned down yet doesn't mean you shouldn't be taking every reasonable precaution to protect yourself against the possibility that it might. Similarly, just because we haven't had many financial scandals yet doesn't mean that we shouldn't be taking steps to minimize both the possibility of it happening and the damage that might result if it did. The fact that your house hasn't yet burned to the ground is no excuse for not having insurance against the unlikely event of it happening the future. The fact that we haven't had many major scandals yet does not constitute proof that the regulations currently in place are good enough.

To make matters worse, national standards require a national consensus. At the time of writing this book, we're only now—in 2016, 149 years after Confederation—making meaningful progress on reducing interprovincial trade barriers. How likely do you think we are to simply get Ontario, Quebec, Alberta, and British Columbia to agree on how to best regulate the investment industry?

Until some of these reforms are fully enacted, Canadian consumers will have to be vigilant in deciding which advisors they work with. Part of the problem is that most people who really should read a book like this one don't because they are too trusting of people they work with and cannot be bothered to look more deeply into the subject. People lead busy lives. Part of why people hire advisors is to take their financial concerns off their plate by handing the management of them over to someone they believe is more knowledgeable and reasonably trustworthy so that they don't have to worry about them anymore.

Improving disclosure should have two primary aims: 1) to maximize consumer understanding of what it is they are buying, and 2) to ensure product suitability. The potential benefits are substantial. They include the following:

- Getting investors to understand that neither products nor any associated advice is free (transparency)

- Allowing both advisors and investors to substitute higher-cost products with lower-cost products (cost arbitrage)
- Allowing for greater potential deductibility depending on the nature of the account
- Removing compensation-induced bias
- Enhancing consumer confidence in both advisor motives and the advice that advisors give
- Improving consumer understanding of the component parts of product costs
- Allowing for a scalability of fees (i.e., volume discount) as accounts grow

The Fiduciary Question

One area where there's been a lively debate lately is regarding the question of whether or not Canada should adopt a fiduciary standard. To date, advisors in Canada have only been required to make recommendations that are "suitable for their clients" and to meet the standard of care owed to the clients, which is not necessarily in their best interests. At issue here are few related matters: the potential increase in the standard of care that advisors (and their firms) are to be held to, the degree to which investors should rely on advisors, and the liabilities associated with providing advice that is appropriate but not necessarily the best. Should the standard of care in Canada be raised? There are two schools of thought.

Ellen Bessner, a prominent securities lawyer who consistently acts on behalf of advisors in court proceedings, wrote the definitive book on advisor risk management, entitled *Advisor at Risk*. In her opinion, owing to the development of the Canadian legal system, a move to the fiduciary standard in Canada in some instances already exists. Her position is as follows:

> Canadian law is well settled and already protects clients who can prove that their advisors (doctors, lawyers, accountants, and FSPs) were negligent or breached their contract. However, if a client can prove that the relationship was elevated to a fiduciary level by proving that they reposed their trust and confidence in the advisor and were vulnerable, a fiduciary duty will exist [Hodgkinson v. Simms, (1994) 3 S.C.R. 377 (S.C.C.)]. Not all client-advisor relationships are fiduciary because clients may be quite sophisticated and involved in decisions made on the account—those clients should not be entitled to an elevated level of protection, particularly when those clients are often the author of their own misfortune by insisting on aggressive strategies that are against the advisor's advice [see Parent v. Leach, (2008) O.J. No. 2155].[43]

Meanwhile, Paul Bates is a former commissioner of the Ontario Securities Commission (OSC), a former CEO of a couple of IIROC member firms, and a current member of Ontario's expert panel looking into granting formal status to advisors in general and financial planners in particular. He believes that the fiduciary standard should be adopted. His view is as follows:

> We should look closely at a proposal put forward by the UK Financial Services Consumer Panel that articulates specific conditions for engagement when in a fiduciary relationship: no conflict of interest; no profit at the expense of the customer without their knowledge or consent; undivided loyalty to the consumer; and a duty of confidentiality. By becoming specific in terms of one's commitment to the client, perhaps in the form of a mutually signed agreement, the nature of exactly what kind of relationship exists would serve both provider and customer well.[44]

Once again, it is Ontario that has taken a leadership role. In its 2016 statement of priorities, the OSC stated that it plans to hold consultations on reforms to registration rules designed to "improve the advisor-client relationship." The paper is clear that the CRM reforms are not the end of retail regulatory reform.[45]

The CSA seems to be of the general opinion that current rules simply aren't good enough. They released a consultation paper on the subject in the spring of 2016. Submissions are still being forwarded, but there are indications that regulators intend to proceed with an implementation plan before March 31, 2017, in order to "better align the interests of registrants to the interests of their clients, to improve outcomes for clients, and to clarify the nature of the client-registrant relationship...." Holding advisors to some sort of fiduciary obligation seems very much in the cards. Parallel reforms have already been enacted in the US. The United States Department of Labor introduced a similar rule that goes into effect in April 2017, although firms have until January 1, 2018, to fully comply.

As it stands, there are already some advisors who are undeniably fiduciaries and others who clearly are not. Anyone who is a portfolio manager or an associate portfolio manager is a fiduciary, for instance. Part of why I elected to become a portfolio manager in 2011 is because I wanted to be held to a higher standard. The test is one of trust and discretion. There is a trust relationship in place where the advisor has the discretion to place trades without having consulted the client beforehand.

Certain organizations such as the Financial Planning Standards Council (FPSC) have gone right up to the line without crossing it. In other words, the FPSC has gone on record to say that CFPs are held to the same standard that fiduciaries are even if a traditional trust relationship is not formally in place. The FPSC's insistence that CFPs use letters of engagement for all client relationships is an example of the mandatory codification of the relationship that the organization feels is an important part of true professionalism.

This strategic move to require all CFPs to put their clients' interests first seems like a motherhood position at first blush. Beneath that surface, however, something far more contentious lurks. The interplay between the considerations of transparency, client interest, informed consent, conflicts of interest, and evidence-based research is coming to the surface. Law professor Mary Condon is a former commissioner of the OSC. In a recent piece in *Investment Executive*, she wrote the following:

> The debate about whether or not to introduce a best interest standard is not only a regulatory debate; it also is a debate about the nature of the industry. The standard is about professionalism, culture, and values—within each organization and industry-wide. The standard is also about saying what you do and doing what you say.[46]

At issue is the concern for consumer protection. Polls consistently show that most Canadians think their advisor has a fiduciary obligation toward them when in fact they do not. When things go wrong, as they sometimes do, these same people are often shocked to learn that all their advisor had to do was recommend products and strategies they deemed "suitable" for their client's circumstances. To my mind, this is about managing both liabilities and expectations, pure and simple.

Sometimes change might not come the way we expect it. If Canada were to adopt a fiduciary standard and it then became generally accepted that anyone held to a fiduciary standard also needed to recommend low-cost products where available, some of the elements of STANDUP advice would be legislated into existence through the back door. It should go without saying that if you're a consumer and you want that particular standard of care, you should seek out an advisor who provides it. For a majority of clients, it's not likely a deal-breaker, but it is another valid consideration in determining whether or not an advisor is right for you.

Not everyone agrees that a fiduciary standard would be such a good thing. Ian Russell, the head of the Investment Industry Association of Canada (IIAC), the trade association for securities dealers, once told me that "if you impose a hard fiduciary standard on IIROC firms, you might as well shut the industry." My bias has always been to protect consumers; Ian's mandate is to represent the interests of member firms. Most consumers want a fiduciary standard and are surprised that it doesn't actually exist. Meanwhile, most advisors I talk to are stringently opposed to it. It's just another example of the ongoing push/pull of regulatory reform.

What cannot be disputed is that the financial advice industry is consolidating. According to an IIAC newsletter published in July 2016, twenty-eight small institutional firms and thirty-five retail firms have exited the business in the four years ending on June 30, 2016. There's no doubt in my mind that if advisory standards were strengthened from "standard of care" to "fiduciary standard," many advisors would be forced to exit the industry as firms closed their doors, as a number of those advisors would have nowhere to go. To my mind, this would be a positive development. I'd call it financial services Darwinism brought about by a regulatory survival of the fittest. My view remains that if the business of advice were to become more of a meritocracy, it would create a bump in credibility. Far from creating an advice gap, I believe higher standards would enhance advisor quality to overcome the value gap.

As such, whenever I have discussions with advisors about where the industry is headed, I get a pretty good feel for how good the advisor I'm talking to really is. The more defensive the advisor, the more likely I am to suspect a lack of competency. They engage in scare-monger tactics about an advice gap to justify their own existence. Here's a specific example. A few years ago, the primary test of suitability was framed by the letters "KYC," which stand for "Know Your Client." These days, there is a parallel obligation called "KYP," or "Know Your Product." The KYP standard was developed because many advisors have been deemed liable to make unsuitable product recommendations if they didn't really understand the products they were recommending to their clients. It has been established that relying solely on a firm's compliance department is insufficient for an advisor who needs to do proper due diligence on the products they recommended to retail clients. If things went wrong, questionable suitability could be linked to an advisor's inability to grasp the full range of possible outcomes associated with a product's value proposition.

The good news in all of this is that the standards associated with giving advice are rising. The question that remains is whether they're rising quickly enough. For advisors who want to be ahead of the curve by instituting the standards of STANDUP advice even if regulators do not currently require them do so, it might be possible to benefit from doing things that go above and beyond what the industry currently requires. Advisory firms should be happy to have leading-edge and highly compliant advisors. Meanwhile, advisors could feel good about the work they do and the services they offer by being the trailblazers of professionalism. Finally, retail clients would likely be a fair bit happier working with someone who goes beyond industry norms regarding transparency and alignment. Whenever someone polls the investing public, they find high levels of support for the introduction of a fiduciary standard. In short, open-ended inquiries seem to suggest that Canadians both

A. like and trust their existing advisors; and
B. would like to see a fiduciary standard implemented (when advised of its absence after the fact).

Here's another example of just how widely the concept of clients' best interests might extend and of how the choice architecture of putting options expressly on the table forces more rewarding conversations. In Australia, regulatory reforms have made it mandatory for advisors to ask their clients about socially responsible investing (SRI). This inquiry must now be verified via a checkbox on the new client application form (i.e., it must be checked off one way or another). Feedback has suggested that this one simple yet actionable reform has led to a material increase in the awareness of (and use of) SRI options. This strikes me as being entirely sensible. People cannot be expected to ask for product options if they do not know that those options exist. To my mind, the only way regulators can be confident that there was informed consent is to have a written record of it.

Tailored Approach

The Ontario government has recently indicated a desire to explore taking a more tailored approach to regulating financial planning. I attended both roundtable sessions on the subject and took careful notes. Some stakeholders mistakenly used the terms *planner* and *advisor* interchangeably. Once again, this is a common mistake. *Planner* refers to people who engage in an activity that can only be performed once, demonstrating a technical competency while adhering to a code of ethics. *Advisor* refers to people who have a licence to sell a product, be it insurance, mutual funds, securities, or some combination of those. People can be one, the other, both, or neither. For example, IIROC advisors also have a code of ethics.

A representative from Advocis made helpful comments that demonstrated the overlapping Venn diagram of advisors in general and of planners in particular. The first thing that we need to determine, therefore, is the scope and applicability of whatever regulations are enacted. I have concluded that, in my opinion, it would be best if we simply regulated financial planners and not all registrants (licensed advisors).

The best way to do this is likely to recognize only one true high standard. Fortuitously, we have that already in the Certified Financial Planner (CFP) designation. I believe that new regulations—and ultimately professional status—should apply only to the approximately nine thousand CFPs currently practicing in Ontario. If this were to happen, I believe other provinces in English Canada would follow suit. (Currently, Quebec is the only province that has legislation in place to regulate financial planning activities.) My view is that since the impetus for this initiative is the dual mandate of consumer protection and the primacy of retirement income, there is a real risk to the public if less qualified people are allowed to call themselves qualified planners.

Paul Bates is one of the people on the committee looking into regulating financial advice in Ontario. At a public meeting in the summer of 2016, he stated that he thinks we need to

A. not add a materially new level of bureaucracy; and
B. use the current regulators (those in charge of licensure) on the presumption that they are essentially doing a good job already.

The preliminary report for Ontario suggested that we establish a new body—the Financial Services Regulatory Authority (FSRA)—to provide oversight for fee-only planners, since they have no licence and therefore their employers do not provide regulatory oversight. Given that this would actually add another layer of bureaucracy, I disagree with the practicality of the first point and almost entirely disagree with the premise of the second. I must stress that these are early days and that I am simply voicing my concern regarding an ongoing discussion.

If we need to create something new, such as the FSRA, then we're adding to the bureaucracy. Conversely, getting the FPSC to do the regulation does not create anything new; it repurposes something that's already in place (and captures all CFPs without adding anything new). Also, it is my experience that some of the firms currently employing advisors (both CFPs and others who consider themselves "planners" but without the CFP designation) have no experience in monitoring and regulating financial planning. Forcing smaller dealers to add this skill set will only cause more small firms to merge due to the ongoing high cost of regulatory compliance. This is a potential unintended consequence that I don't think the panel has considered, and I simply don't see how small or even medium-sized firms are qualified to perform this role.

At the same public hearing, Andrew Kriegler, the head of IIROC, stated his concern about possible regulatory arbitrage, a concern that I share. He fears that different self-regulating organizations (SROs) will enforce rules unevenly in order to give their registrants an advantage. I would add that this could occur even if it is not deliberate. Some organizations simply have more of a capacity to ensure compliance than others. In my opinion, it is easier and better to morph a single, pre-existing but consistent and overarching certification body into a regulator than it is to morph three pre-existing product-centric "regulators"—with a currently non-existent fourth one to be added—into something that maintains a consistently high standard and protects consumers. Having one set of rules but four separate regulators enforcing them is, to my mind, a recipe for disaster.

Given what we discussed in Part 1, I believe the answer is obvious. Some planners work at brokerages, some work at insurance agencies, and some work at their own fee-for-service firms with no additional employer or oversight. If we were to leave the task of regulating planning to the existing regulators, we'd likely have a disparate series of approaches and applications, and we'd also have to create an additional regulatory body just to regulate the planners who have no licenses to sell products. I believe it is simpler, cheaper, and more consistent to have the FPSC regulate financial planning activity in Canada.

Titles

The titles that advisors can use are also finally receiving some attention. There are dozens. Most of them are essentially made up and designed to seem more impressive or specialized than they actually are. To date, there has been no meaningful regulation on what advisors can call themselves. As such, some advisors come up with their own versions of titles and, unless their employer has a policy on the subject, usually end up being allowed to use it. There needs to be greater clarity on what products and services clients can reasonably expect from advisors they approach.

From a consumer protection perspective—not to mention truth in advertising and reputational risk perspectives—this needs to stop. Whether the restrictions and clarity are brought about by regulation (internally) or legislation (externally), there is an obvious need for an entire industry to come to terms with what its participants can reasonably call themselves. This is a specific concern regarding financial planning. Except for company-specific policies, there is currently nothing prohibiting someone who has no express background in financial planning from calling themselves a financial planner in English Canada.

Deductibility of Investment Counselling Fees

The tax deductibility of investment counselling fees is a poorly understood and often improperly quantified benefit that already exists within the industry. In essence, the tax deduction associated with a separate, unbundled fee is (where applicable) a similar tax deduction to the one embedded in the product. It is simply calculated in slightly a different way, which I will discuss later.

The Income Tax Act allows for the deductibility of investment counselling fees under Section 20 (1) (bb). The prevailing view is that financial planning fees (e.g., those associated with a financial independence calculation and illustration) are not deductible. As a result, many advisors have taken to doing their financial planning work for free, provided the investment counselling fees are sufficiently large. The problem is that professional counselling fees are only deductible if they do not apply to registered accounts. Counselling fees for registered plans (RRSPs, RRIFs, LIRAs, RESPs, etc.) are not tax deductible. Only the fees associated with non-registered accounts (also known as cash accounts or investment accounts) are tax deductible. If a consumer has both an investment account and a registered account with an advisor, the deductibility is prorated and allowed on a proportional basis. There are many people who feel the Income Tax Act needs to be revised in order to clarify the issue of deductibility of financial planning fees and whether deductions should be allowed when F-class mutual funds are used.

Since fees for advice regarding securities trading (whether discretionary or non-discretionary) are potentially deductible while commissions are certainly not deductible, there is also a minor debate regarding "free" transactions in a fee-based account. Some firms allow households a certain number of trades based on overall asset levels, while others insist on modest cost-recovery charges (e.g., $20 per trade) in order to separate transaction charges from advisory fees. Some accounting firms take the position that, in order to be entirely and unambiguously compliant with CRA's intent, the inclusion of "free trades" has real costs that, while modest, could compromise the deductibility of the totality of any fee. The expectation by CRA, they say, is to reduce fees modestly and to charge separately for transactions to remove any doubt about possible "transaction subsidies" offered in the form of free trades.

Both opponents and proponents of direct fees have likely misrepresented tax deductibility at one time or another. Opponents say that since there is a de facto deduction through the taxable reduction of gains in an MER, there is no benefit in deducting fees separately. This is true only if they're talking about instruments that earn dividend and capital gains income. Conversely, proponents imply that the benefit of the deduction is absolute and applies in all circumstances. This, too, is erroneous.

It is true that products with embedded compensation already offer a deduction through the reduced income or capital gains realized through MER deductions. This reality is ignored by some advisors who overstate the benefits of deductibility in the furtherance of making a sale. A $100,000 investment in a bond fund that earns 3.0% minus the cost of an embedded 0.50% trailing commission leads to $2,500 in taxable income at the client's top marginal rate in a cash account. If the same fund is used in an F-class format and an identical fee is charged, there is no benefit to the consumer from a tax perspective because the deduction occurs at the same marginal tax and inclusion rates.

What about vehicles earning capital gains? The capital gains inclusion rate of 50% and the taxation work the same way. When funds prepare T3 tax returns, they first deduct MER expenses against interest income. They then deduct any remaining MER expenses against dividend income, and if there is any further remainder, they deduct it against capital gains. They do this to maximize unitholder tax benefits.

Make Financial Planning Tax-Deductible

I am a portfolio manager (PM) with an IIROC registration. As such, the fees I charge are clearly tax deductible (for non-registered accounts). That's because investment counselling fees are deductible under the federal Income Tax Act (ITA) Section 20 (1) (bb). The ITA has considerable precedent in case law showing that investment counselling fees are tax deductible but transactional commissions are not. Some tax advisors have said that no matter how nominal a transactional charge might be, it should be charged, lest the implied cost of the transaction might taint the full deductibility of a fee.

For example, say a client had $1 million in a taxable account attracting a 1.0% ($10,000) annual fee. Let's further assume that this client executed thirteen trades in the most recent calendar year. What would those trades have cost if conducted in a transactional account? No matter how nominal, the value is certainly not $0. No one would take a client, charge $0 in commissions, and have the firm incur some transaction charges (execution commissions) to do those thirteen trades. Commissions are not deductible. If the client were to pay the 1.0% fee and then a separate $20 transaction charge, that would be fine. However, if the value of those same trades were deemed to be $20 per trade, then $260 might be subtracted from the deductible portion of the client's fee, making only $9,740 deductible. Commissions are not deductible, even if you give them away as a loss leader.

What about financial planning? It is not expressly referenced in the ITA. Considering the transactional example above, I can tell you that many of my colleagues at other firms have presently taken to giving away their financial plans as loss leaders when providing investment counselling services. By including it in their comprehensive investment counselling fee, they effectively include something that shouldn't ever be legally deductible into a different line item that sometimes is legally deductible. This practice is unlikely to be caught in CRA audits. Note also that the majority of these portfolio managers are not likely CFPs.

Financial planning services are currently not tax deductible. I have been told privately that the lack of standardized regulation is the primary reason why governments (both federal and provincial) have not allowed for financial planning services to be deductible to date. If the rationale for not allowing deductibility is that the activity is not reasonably regulated, it stands to reason that the associated services should be deductible if those services were regulated down the road.

Making financial planning fees tax deductible has many benefits. If consumers were to see that the fees associated with financial planning services are deductible, it would both underscore the legitimacy of the activity and make it more affordable to the ordinary people who need it. It is unlikely that people will perceive the value of a service if there is no line item on a statement that expressly quantifies its value. Lastly, it would be a lot easier for do-it-yourself investors and all the people who will be coping with the alleged "advice gap" to afford financial planning advice if they could deduct the costs associated with it.

People respond to incentives. Today, most people who want financial planning get it sporadically as a loss leader from people whose primary source of income is offering advice on regulated investment products. In my home province of Ontario, there are perhaps a thousand CFPs who do not hold a single licence to sell securities, mutual funds, or insurance. My sense is that these are generally among the best, brightest, and most underused planners in the province—they must add value in order to earn a living, and they do not supplement their income by placing products.

Making financial planning tax deductible would create a virtuous circle whereby planners can differentiate themselves and find better, more desirable clients by virtue of their value-adding skill set. Consumers can find comfort in knowing that they are working with a qualified professional. The benefits are likely to be significant and accumulative for everyone concerned.

The irony in all of this is that the ITA allows for deductions for services involving investment counselling, something that is largely the domain of the so-called "1%." Meanwhile, financial planning services are not tax deductible to anyone under any circumstances. I wonder if Prime Minister Trudeau and Finance Minister Morneau are thinking about this. In the autumn of 2015, the federal Liberals campaigned on a platform that included a tax cut for "those who are in the middle class and those who are working hard to join it." This resulted in a tax savings of up to about $670 for the highest-earning middle class citizens. At the same time, much to the dismay of many people I know in my line of work, the federal government also brought in a tax hike of 4% on all earned income above $200,000. Once we have proper regulation for financial planning in Canada (and that shouldn't take too long), a strong argument could be made that the next logical step would be to make financial planning services tax deductible so that ordinary Canadians can benefit from the same sorts of tax breaks that, at least until recently, have benefited the top 1% of income earners.

CHAPTER 17
BE A STANDUP ADVISOR

I have a dream…and any advisor who is serious about being a STANDUP advisor needs to get with the program. The train is leaving the station. This means implementing as many of the best practices employed by other professionals as soon as possible. It means getting credentials that demonstrate a capacity to offer advice and no longer making do with merely having licences to sell products. It means talking to clients frankly to explain how the industry is changing and that positive, necessary, and long-overdue reforms are coming. Most of all, it means that advisors will need to put consumer interests ahead of personal and corporate interests in a way that is clear, persuasive, and unimpeachable.

As stakeholders become more comfortable with how the industry works and what needs to change, trailblazing advisors will be rewarded. More than ever, the good advisors are winning. Newly informed consumers will gravitate toward advisors who demonstrate true professionalism.

There's absolutely nothing stopping advisors from continuing to do business the way they have throughout their entire lives, and no one has to change anything if they don't want to (yet). That's the funny thing about change—it will occur whether you want it to or not. Resisting it usually just means less pain sooner and more pain later. Advisors need to decide whether they want to jump now or be pushed later.

The Professionalism Payoff

By diverting energy from sales pitches toward activities that society views as being truly representative of professionalism, we could get to a clear win-win situation for both clients and advisors. Imagine a world where STANDUP advisors win out precisely because they are conspicuously good.

The method of compensating an advisor doesn't indicate either the existence of ethics or a lack of ethics in and of itself. The real issues are concerning questions of cost consciousness, evidence-based recommendations, and informed consent. Compensation considerations can skew the recommendations advisors make, and bias, including the perception of bias, obviously still exists. But to the extent that we could alter this perception, why wouldn't we all band together to do it?

If there is one thing that has come across loud and clear in my conversations with most consumers over the years, it is that they are quite open to working with an advisor they can trust to look out for their best interests. As it stands now, many are skeptical. A cynic might even say that the few consumers of financial products and advice who are not skeptical are naive.

Wouldn't it be great if consumers were neither of those things and were justifiably content? Wouldn't it be absolutely fantastic if consumers trusted advisors implicitly because the way they went about doing their work was transparent, aligned with the clients' highest values, and the highest quality in terms of both competence and ethics?

Clearly, advisors want to be thought of as professionals. So far, I still don't see enough of a willingness to explain and use both active and passive strategies, as well as the meaningful disclosure regarding the pros and cons of both. We have a chicken and egg situation here. Some advisors tell me they'll explain both options if clients ask them to. Most clients are oblivious to the evidence and don't ask about it. As a result, most advisors never get around to explaining it.

In my opinion, there are things that a STANDUP advisor could do voluntarily and immediately to improve professionalism, trust, and understanding. Since, as the saying goes, "sunshine is the best disinfectant," more disclosure might be preferred to less. Advisors could write this disclosure in terms any competent layperson could understand. It might include the use of letters of engagement, compensation disclosure letters with transparent fees, written investment policy statements (IPSs), and so forth, some of which are still not mandatory for most advisors.

Don't wait for the law to change and compel all advisors to do this. Do it now in order to enjoy an "early-mover advantage." While I believe that consumer protection and balanced commercialism can both be preserved through good regulation, I also believe that we can accomplish these objectives at the advisory level if we take proper care at the outset.

Another way that one might look at disclosure is to apply the Golden Rule as it relates to the financial services industry. Essentially, that means advisors should disclose unto others as they would have others disclose unto them. That might well mean that their disclosure involves not only, for instance, what a product costs but also what the impact of that cost would be on a portfolio of a certain size over a certain time frame, all else being equal. This includes the explicit need to recognize that high-cost investment products need to generate outlier-type performance to justify their use.

One of the most all-encompassing IIROC rules is found in Section 29.7 (1). It says that industry participants are to disclose all material facts pertaining to products and services. When I asked an IIROC manager of business conduct compliance to define the standard more precisely, the representative said, "Materiality is well defined in several places. We expect members to be professionals, able to apply rules reasonably." Given this response—by the way, every answer is a response but not every response is an answer—it seems our securities self-regulating organization (SRO) is hamstrung by the nature of our principles-based approach to rules, which makes general guidance difficult because unique circumstances apply. Different firms, in turn, take it upon themselves to draw different lines regarding disclosures, disclaimers, and such. The perspective they bring to the table will inform their individual corporate policies and procedures regarding product disclosures and practice disclaimers, among other things.

More meaningful disclosure is only one way of showing a concern for client welfare. The situation may be worse than some participants are willing to admit. Some organizations such as the CFA Institute have gone so far as to publish a "Statement of Investor Rights." In the CFA Institute's case, the statement itemizes ten minimum things to expect when working with a financial professional in order to collectively restore trust, respect, and integrity in finance.[47] In fact, a recent CFA/Edelman study showed a significant "trust deficit" within the financial services industry in general and in asset management in particular.[48]

Registration As a Portfolio Manager

There are a few thousand portfolio managers (PMs) registered in Canada. These people work on the behalf of their clients on a discretionary basis. They are also the only advisors in Canada who are unambiguously fiduciaries. There's a test regarding whether or not the relationship is a fiduciary one. Is there one-sided reliance or discretionary authority? If a little old lady hires an advisor and that advisor tries their best to help their client but something nonetheless goes wrong, the judge in the case will look at some factors, including the following:

- How much experience did the client have?
- Did the client rely exclusively on the advisor's recommendations and judgment because she was incapable of making a decision on her own?
- Was the advisor given an opportunity to exercise discretion in some way?

This last point is critical. In any non-discretionary situation, the determination of whether or not an advisor is a fiduciary is made on a case-by-case, line-by-line examination of the facts involving the specific client. In contrast, if the advisor is a PM, they have discretion. Here's a simple depiction of what that means:

Discretion = fiduciary obligation to the client

Stated a bit differently, I have found that perhaps the easiest, clearest, most indisputable way for an advisor to demonstrate a STANDUP mentality is to become a PM. This is yet another functions and relations math exercise. Lots of people who are not PMs are nonetheless STANDUP advisors. However, everyone who is a PM is a STANDUP advisor. There are other benefits that might apply to working with a PM. These are not absolute (i.e., they may vary from firm to firm and from PM to PM), but you should be aware of them at any rate. The benefits of working with a PM are as follows:

- PMs are not paid for transactions (in contrast to some fee-based advisors who might charge and be paid something nominal for trading).

- PMs often have their firms waive things for their clients such as trustee fees.
- PMs have access to a wider range of products. Unless you're an accredited investor, you will not have access to certain products offered via something called an offering memorandum (OM). Products offered via an OM are only for people deemed sophisticated enough based on a variety of potential screens. Anyone working with a PM is working with someone who is obligated to put their clients' interests first and to ensure suitability along the way. As a result, people working with a PM often get access to products and securities they'd never be able to buy otherwise.

Advisor Incorporation

One of the important but less obvious differences between mutual fund (MFDA) registrants, insurance registrants, and those who are securities (IIROC) licensed is that the former two are allowed to incorporate, while the latter are not. This is yet another discrepancy being discussed as a possible agenda item for reform. There's an uneven playing field if only some advisors can incorporate. It represents another potential form of regulatory arbitrage. Note that other, more established professions (law, accounting, etc.) have long allowed their practitioners to incorporate. The permission to do so may end up being tied to the progress made (or not) regarding fiduciary standards.

Many of the people who oppose advisor incorporation do so on the grounds that it might harm investor protection. Presumably, if all advisors were required to put their clients' interests ahead of their own, this concern would disappear.

Pulling It All Together

A higher standard is taking shape—one where advisors must actively recommend what is in their clients' best interests. Note that what is best for one might not be best for another, given the randomness of potential outcomes based on a balance of probabilities as well as on some very personal decisions involving mental accounting, biases, and trade-offs. There's a whole series of sequential considerations to keep in mind as you go through the process of being (for advisors) or finding (for consumers) a STANDUP advisor. To summarize:

- Advisors are increasingly being asked to put their clients' interests first; but
- Clients might not even understand their own best interests; and
- Most clients are unaware of cost considerations; so
- Clients may end up investing using the relatively more expensive products their advisor recommends despite cheaper options being available; even though
- It requires an outlier outcome to justify more expensive options; while

- Behavioural economics shows us that most investors are risk-averse and would likely choose the option that has a lower cost drag if it were offered to them; and
- Using products that aim to track benchmarks or capture risk factors does not diminish an advisor's value; it puts the focus on things that are important.

Whoever said product suppliers should decide what an advisor's advice is worth, anyway? The embedded-compensation system robs advisors of the ability to charge what they believe their advice is worth. Do you think that all advisors believe they are created equal and deserve to be paid equally?

According to the Investment Funds Institute of Canada (IFIC), the trade association promoting mutual funds, Canadians had $1.27 trillion invested in mutual funds as of June 30, 2016.[49] Meanwhile, according to the Canadian ETF Association (CETFA), the trade association for ETFs, Canada surpassed $100 billion in ETFs around the same time.[50] It is estimated that about 33% of Canadian households (4.9 million families) own mutual funds,[51] while only a small fraction of that number own ETFs. Since most mutual funds involve embedded commissions and most ETFs do not, it is important to note recent research completed by Credo Consulting Inc. They completed a large survey of more than two thousand Canadians, and 42% of respondents said they were not paying for advice or were unsure.[52]

To that end, the Financial Consumer Agency of

Canada (FCAC) is in the process of developing a national strategy on financial literacy. A significant part of what they are trying to achieve is to get ordinary people to understand the considerable and often nuanced financial information that can go into decision-making. The FCAC did a study in 2014 and came up with similar results. They determined that many Canadians did not understand advisor compensation, that almost 60% did not know how much wealth they would need to maintain their standard of living in retirement, and that slightly more than a third of Canadians are not saving for retirement whatsoever![53]

Things Don't Always Go According to Plan

Things don't always go according to plan, and there are bound to be some clients who choose to work with an advisor who tells a great story. Sometimes, the best laid plans can go at least a little awry. It reminds me of a story....

Dan was a single guy living at home with his father and working in the family business. When he found out he was going to inherit a fortune when his sickly father died, he decided he needed to find a wife with whom to share his fortune. One evening, he spotted the most beautiful woman he had ever seen. Her natural beauty took his breath away.

"I might look like just an ordinary guy," he said to her, "but in a few months, my father will die, and I will inherit twenty million dollars."

Impressed, the woman asked for his business card, and just three days later…she became his stepmother.

There are perhaps an estimated 140,000 financial advisors in Canada—more than 15,000 are licensed to sell securities, just fewer than 80,000 are licensed to sell mutual funds, and just fewer than 80,000 are licensed to sell insurance. Due to some advisors having multiple licenses, many are double counted, which is why it is difficult to estimate a reliable number.

The best advisors will be set not only to survive but also to thrive like never before—while doing what is best for their clients. The UK's ban on embedded commissions seems to have led to a rapid drop in the sale of products with the highest MERs. Mark Wheatley, the former head of the Financial Conduct Authority (FCA), the UK's national regulator, recently told a Toronto audience that after the ban was imposed in 2013, the highest-cost mutual funds on the market went from about 60% of all products sold to about 20% of all products sold within about six months.[54] I see that as significant progress in saving consumers money. Similarly, James Norris, the managing director of international operations for Vanguard, has recently suggested that "Within a decade, none of the major markets of the world will be using embedded-compensation structures."[55] There is no longer any reasonable doubt that a move to a STANDUP model is accelerating.

Financial advice comes in many shapes and sizes and can encompass a truly mind-boggling array of additional considerations and surprises. The financial advice industry is evolving, but the primary disagreements seem to revolve around how to get to where I believe we are heading.

Isn't this a good time to get all stakeholders involved in a purposeful dialogue about how to get there?

CHAPTER 18
FIND A STANDUP ADVISOR

More than ever, an informed consumer is a good consumer. This ancient proverb is more appropriate today than ever before: "Tell me and I forget. Show me and I remember. Involve me and I understand." Consumers need to get involved. They need to force the other stakeholders to give them more meaningful information for decision-making. These stakeholders need to present this information in a more understandable and accessible manner. Consumers need to look closely and to know in advance what it is they should hope to see. There are already enough advisors in the marketplace who espouse professional principles that finding one shouldn't be difficult. This is particularly important for people who are dissatisfied with their current advisor.

Relationships are predicated on the usual hallmarks of professionalism: honesty, integrity, experience, and a genuine concern for the welfare of the client. If the advisor you're working with today possesses these qualities, you would probably be well advised to stick with that person. Of course, constructively encouraging that advisor to get credentials, unbundle and disclose fees and commissions, and implement a number of professional best practices wouldn't hurt either.

Since an ounce of prevention is worth a pound of cure, disclosure at the point of sale needs to be overhauled and augmented considerably. This is especially true regarding so called "manufactured" investment products: mutual funds, segregated funds, structured notes, and universal life insurance policies.

Consumers need to address the industry's tarnished reputation head on. Concerned stakeholders such as the Small Investor Protection Association (SIPA), the Consumers Council of Canada, CARP (formerly known as the Canadian Association of Retired Persons), and Kenmar Associates have been making helpful suggestions for some time now. These groups use their resources to ensure that consumer interests are heard. Many prominent consumer advocates are also lending a hand.

Reading this book will get most people up to a reasonable basic level of understanding. The problem is that most people simply feel ill-equipped to properly determine whom to work with. This is one of the problems identified in Joseph Stiglitz's research regarding the asymmetry of information. (See Chapter 9.)

How can anyone really do proper due diligence in a field where the people they're interviewing know far more about the subject than they themselves know? This is true with anything: cars, computers, property insurance—you name it. Also, in one last point about the difference between fact and opinion, I recently came across an excellent quote from philosopher

Bertrand Russell, who wrote, "The fact that an opinion has been widely held is no evidence whatever that it is not utterly absurd." Giving advice to retail consumers is not a popularity contest.

I've put together the following questions, which I believe will help most people get the meaningful answers they need when choosing an advisor. I've also included some reasons why they matter.

1. What licences do you hold?

For most advisors, the answer will be one of the following: insurance, mutual funds, or securities. Your licensing as an advisor determines what products you can and cannot recommend to a client. In certain instances, advisors will be licenced to sell two or more product lines. Any advisor with a securities licence is automatically licenced to sell mutual funds.

2. What is your opinion of the products that you are *not* licenced to sell?

This is a first-derivative sort of question. The answer to Question 1 is factual. The answer to Question 2 is attitudinal. You're looking for attitudes and limitations that the advisor might ultimately use to justify certain recommendations. Remember, when you're good with a hammer....

3. What designations do you hold?

You're looking for a commitment to continuing education above and beyond the minimum required to hold a licence. In general, any designation is proof of that commitment. Beware or designations that you've never heard of, since they may be the questionable and basic sorts designed to suggest legitimacy. In my view, for most retail clients, the most qualified designation is Certified Financial Planner (CFP).

4. How long have you been an advisor, and will I be working directly with you or just a member of your team?

There are no unambiguously right or wrong answers, but there are instructive ones. Newer advisors are usually younger, more eager, more service-oriented (since they have fewer clients, they have fewer client demands), and more willing to take on smaller accounts. More experienced advisors sometimes give certain tasks to staff (which could be either good or bad, depending on the quality of staff and your personal perspective) and have higher minimums. Still, they may generally know the ropes better than people who have been in the business for three years or less. The follow-up question is mostly for the sake of clarity. Just be aware of what you're signing on for.

5. How would you describe your commitment to your clients?

This is a gut-check question. Does it pass the test? Does the answer seem sincere? Is it actionable? Returning all phone calls within two hours sounds implausible—twenty-four hours is more likely. Listen carefully to the answer and follow up by asking for specific examples.

6. What would you say is the importance of minimizing product cost?
You're trying to ferret out the opinion of the advisor you're interviewing. This is, to my mind, one of the very best ways of determining if the person you're speaking to is a STANDUP advisor. At the very least— and irrespective of the advisor's preferred business model—the advisor should acknowledge that cost is important. If they change the subject and start talking exclusively about "value" or some such thing, while ignoring cost, you should be worried. Other things that you can ask about include asset allocation and tax minimization (both important) as well as security/fund selection and market timing (both unimportant). These determinations about relative importance are personal, but I stand by my opinions.

7. What would you say is the importance of past performance in choosing products or securities?
There's a reason why prospectuses say you shouldn't rely on past performance. Nonetheless, the evidence is clear that past performance doesn't predict future performance. Since we cannot rely on past performance, please stop relying on it.

8. How do you ascertain a client's risk level, and what do you do to manage it?

Most people focus on (expected) returns exclusively, but risk is equally important. It's the flip side of the same coin. You won't get returns if you can't stay invested long enough to get them because you can't handle the associated risk. At any rate, the advisor should have a good risk profile questionnaire that all clients answer before opening an account. Open-ended questions (both ways) are good for getting more perspective on these sorts of "soft" issues.

9. What kind of returns should I expect?

For a balanced investor (say, 30% income; 70% stocks) and in the context of current market conditions, something in the neighbourhood of 5% to 6% is a reasonable return expectation. Conservative investors can take off 1.0% to 1.5%; aggressive ones can add 1.0% to 1.5%. If anyone ever suggests an expectation (even for an all-stock investor) in the double-digit range is reasonable, you should be highly doubtful.

10. Does the return expectation take inflation, account fees, and account expenses into account?

The numbers in Question 9 assume inflation of 2% and are cited before advisory costs (be they in the form of fees or commissions) and product costs. In other words, the numbers above likely overstate expected returns by the amount of associated costs. If the sum of the product and advice cost of your portfolio is 2%, you should shave an additional 2% off your expected return. Note that if you pay advisory expenses outside of your portfolio, the case could be made that this cost could be excluded.

11. What can you tell me about behavioural finance (a.k.a. behavioural economics)?

Hopefully, the advisor will be aware of this critically important field. If a primary part of an advisor's job description is behavioural coaching, they should at least be aware of what quirks to watch out for.

12. Where do you get your financial news and information?

There are plenty of sources of information, but the real question you're trying to have answered is whether the advisor is an investment pornographer. If their information is based on short-term movements, forecasts, and almost instantly obsolete company research reports, be worried. If the advisor reads more generally about long-term trends, tries to stay abreast of public policy changes (TFSA limits, for example), and gets their ideas based on verified evidence from learned journals and universities, you should feel assured.

13. How would you describe your ideal client and your typical client? (There's a difference.)

Hopefully, it'll sound a fair bit like you…what your circumstances are and what you're looking for.

14. How much money do you manage and how many clients are in your client base?

This is a way of verifying the typical client aspect in Question 13. It's simple math: 200 clients and $20 million under management means an average household asset level of $100,000; 100 clients and $50 million under management means an average asset level of $500,000. You likely don't want to be way (100%) higher or way (50%) lower than the average asset value. In other words, if an advisor's average client account is $250,000, you might begin to worry if you have over $500,000 or under $125,000 to invest.

15. Do you consider yourself a fiduciary?
This is a bit of a trick question since the only Canadian advisors currently held to a fiduciary standard are those who are registered as portfolio managers (PMs), and there are only about three thousand PMs in Canada. Go back to Questions 5 and 6 and probe for more clarity. In the US, for instance, there is legislation that is about to take effect that suggests that part of being a fiduciary involves paying strict attention to product costs. If the advisor claims to be (or even simply to think like) a fiduciary, yet seems indifferent to product cost, you will have uncovered a misrepresentation of sorts.

16. What additional services do you provide and how do you charge for them? Is there anything you cannot do for me?
The answers here are more situational than they are right or wrong. Be sure that the person you're hiring

can do what you want done. Also, you should be clear that there might be limitations to what your advisor can do. Beyond basic general direction and unless you are a lawyer, you should not reasonably expect your advisor to be up to speed on the nuances of provincial family law, for instance.

17. How and how much do you charge? Can I get that in writing?

We've looked at advisory compensation earlier. Is the advisor in the right ballpark given your account size and what you're expecting them to do for you? Anything that is not crystal clear should worry you.

18. Do you use a letter of engagement (LOE)?

It is good to have a formal, signed document that codifies exactly what the advisor will and will not do on your behalf. You can avoid many misunderstandings by getting details in writing at the outset. I might add that the FPSC Code of Ethics requires that all CFPs have an LOE on file for all clients. Therefore, a CFP who does not use an LOE is out of compliance.

19. Where do you stand on the active/passive debate?

You're looking for a sensible answer here. There are no unambiguously right or wrong answers, but if the advisor takes this as an opening to tout one of the approaches without reasonably depicting the attributes of both, there's a cause for concern. Good advisors help their clients see the pros and cons associated with competing alternatives and help them find what works best for them. Personal opinions are fine as long as they're balanced and evidence-based.

20. How do you help clients choose between competing alternatives?

As with Question 19, you're testing for how doctrinaire the advisor is. In the majority of situations, the best solution is the one that works for you, the client. If you ever get the sense that the advisor offers cookie-cutter solutions, you should quite properly wonder about how customized and personalized their advice really is. This applies to both products and strategies.

21. What specifically did you recommend to your clients during the global financial crisis of 2008–2009?

You're looking for consistency here. STANDUP advisors generally told clients to stay the course, and in some cases they resisted pressure from both clients and compliance departments to reduce exposure to growth assets. Many others timed markets (or at least tried to) and generally went "off message" in political speak. You're looking for an advisor who says what they mean and does what they say they're going to do…with a track record to validate it.

22. How often do you rebalance your clients' portfolios?

The simple right answer to the rebalancing question is that the advisor consistently does it. In short, you're not really asking about secret formulae regarding operational procedures. Rather, you're asking the advisor to verify a commitment to doing what the research shows usually improves risk-adjusted returns—the "how" is secondary. What's important is that they abide by Nike's famous slogan: "Just do it."

Also, here is a question that, in my opinion, is useless:

Can I speak with a few clients like me?
Why this doesn't work: Cherry-picked referrals don't really offer much of anything useful. Do you believe infomercials? Random testimonials? How is this different, really? Every client has a different set of wants, needs, and means.

What Else Can You Do?
In the end, change will come. If we sit back, it will continue to evolve slowly. However, if we take action, it might come more quickly. It only seems reasonable to choose the second path since the finality of the outcome seems so inevitable. Practically speaking, we're now at the point where the Canadian Securities Administrators (CSA) seems to agree on where we're going.

There is an old saying that persists today suggesting that knowledge is power. I disagree somewhat. I believe knowledge only becomes truly powerful when combined with deliberate, purposeful action. The time has come for everyone involved to put their knowledge into action and come to terms with the changes that will be necessary to move the rendering of financial advice forward into the realm of a true profession.

There are those who believe that various forms of malfeasance will not go away and that meaningful dispute resolution is still unavailable. Some advisors are still unaware of the existence of their own arbitration rights, alternative dispute resolution options, and potential recourses offered by the Ombudsman for Banking Services and Investments (OBSI). There are many consumer advocates who would suggest that the pursuit of justice through these means is ineffective anyway, given how few complaints result in rulings that favour consumers. The industry is not seen as being responsive to repeated pleas for increased and improved consumer protection.

A related matter regarding both disclosure and the improvement of the advisor-client relationship is performance reporting. The industry has long resisted giving clients a personal annualized rate of return on statements. The stated reason for the resistance is that the mathematics is cumbersome and that systems data, particularly when accounts transfer from other dealers, is incomplete. This difficulty is why performance reporting will be the last element of the Client Relationship Model (CRM) to be implemented.

There are more than a few skeptics who fear that

the real reason behind this suppression of individualized performance reporting is that most companies and advisors do not want to be held accountable for performance that lags benchmarks. I am one of those skeptics. I remain confident that performance reporting will greatly enhance trust and understanding once it becomes mandatory. That said, let's all recognize that the reporting might cost more and that those costs might be passed on to investors. In the meantime, www.getsmarteraboutmoney.com, the website run by the Investor Education Fund of the Ontario Securities Commission (OSC), not only lets people plug in real-world data to derive customized return data, albeit with a very limited application (provided you also correctly input your cost data); it also features a wide range of useful tools and calculators to help people help themselves.

We're all in this together. Consumers should demand more. Product manufacturers and distributors can do more. Politicians can do more. Regulators can do more. Enforcement officials can do more. It's time for all stakeholders to step up to the plate and show a real commitment to converting this sales-cultured business into a real profession.

This is a call to action. If you are involved in the financial services industry in any way, do not simply put this book down and move on with your life. Instead, do something to encourage meaningful change in an industry that desperately needs to continue to embrace substantive change in order to become a true profession.

If you really care about the future of financial advice in Canada, here are some groups you can to contact to help effect positive change:

Provincial Regulators

Alberta Securities Commission
    403-297-6454, 1-877-355-0585
    www.albertasecurities.com
Alberta Insurance Council
    780-421-4148 (Edmonton)
    403-233-2929 (Calgary)
    www.abcouncil.ab.ca
British Columbia Securities Commission
    604-899-6500, 1-800-373-6393
    www.bcsc.bc.ca
Insurance Council of British Columbia
    604-688-0321,
    1-877-688-0321 (toll-free within BC)
    www.insurancecouncilofbc.com
Manitoba Securities Commission
    204-945-2548
    1-800-655-5244 (toll-free within Manitoba)
    www.mbsecurities.ca
Manitoba Justice Consumer Protection Division
    204-945-3744, 1-866-626-4862
    www.gov.mb.ca/cca/
Insurance Council of Manitoba
    204-988-6800
    www.icm.mb.ca
New Brunswick Financial and Consumer Services

Commission

1-866-933-2222

www.fcnb.ca

New Brunswick Consumer Advocate for Insurance,

506-549-5555, 1-888-283-5111

www.insurance-assurance.ca

Newfoundland and Labrador Financial Services Regulation Division

709-729-4189

www.servicenl.gov.nl.ca/securities/

Newfoundland and Labrador Insurance Regulation Division

709-729-2602

www.servicenl.gov.nl.ca/insurance/

Nova Scotia Securities Commission

902-424-7768,

1-855-424-2499 (toll-free within Nova Scotia)

nssc.novascotia.ca

Nova Scotia Financial Institutions Division

902-424-6331

www.novascotia.ca/finance/en/home/financialservices/

Ontario Securities Commission

416-593-8314, 1-877-785-1555

www.osc.gov.on.ca

Financial Services Commission of Ontario

416-250-7250, 1-800-668-0128

www.fsco.gov.on.ca

Northwest Territories Securities Office

1-867-767-9305

www.justice.gov.nt.ca/en/divisions/legal-registries-division/securities-office/

Northwest Territories Superintendent of Insurance
867-767-9177 ext. 15250, 1-800-661-0820
www.fin.gov.nt.ca/services/insurance-licensing-regulation

Nunavut Legal Registries
867-975-6590
www.nunavutlegalregistries.ca

Autorité des marchés financiers (AMF) (Quebec financial regulation)
514-395-0337, 1-877-525-0337
www.lautorite.qc.ca/

PEI Office of the Superintendent of Securities
902-368-4551
www.gov.pe.ca/securities/

PEI Superintendent of Insurance
902-368-4550

Saskatchewan Financial and Consumer Affairs Authority, Securities Division
306-787-5645,
1-877-880-5550 (toll-free in Saskatchewan)
www.fcaa.gov.sk.ca/Securities%20Division

Saskatchewan Financial and Consumer Affairs Authority, Consumer Protection Division
306-787-5550

Yukon Office of the Superintendent of Securities
867-667-5466, 1-800-661-0408 (toll-free in Yukon)
www.community.gov.yk.ca/corp/securities_about.html

Yukon Superintendent of Insurance
867-667-5940

Miscellaneous Financial Services Contacts

Advocis
416-444-5251, 1-800-563-5822
www.advocis.ca

Canada Deposit Insurance Corporation
1-800-461-2342
www.cdic.ca

Canadian Institute of Financial Planners
647-723-6445 ext. 134, 1-866-933-0233 ext. 134
www.cifps.ca

Canadian Securities Institute
416-364-9130, 1-866-866-2601
www.csi.ca

Canadian Life and Health Insurance Association
1-888-295-8112, 416-777-9002 (Toronto)
514-282-2088 (Montreal)
www.clhia.ca

Certified General Accountants,
1-800-663-1529
www.cga-canada.org

Chartered Professional Accountants of Canada
416-977-0748, 1-800-268-3793
www.cica.ca

Financial Planning Standards Council
416-593-8587, 1-800-305-9886
www.fpsc.ca

Insurance Brokers Association of Canada
416-367-1831
www.ibac.ca

Investment Funds Institute of Canada

416-363-2150, 1-866-347-1961

www.ific.ca

Investment Industry Regulatory Organization of Canada

416-364-6133, 1-877-442-4322

www.iiroc.ca

Investor Learning Centre

www.investorlearning.ca

Kenmar Associates

416-244-5803

Montréal Exchange

514-871-2424, 1-800-361-5353

www.m-x.ca

Mutual Fund Dealers Association of Canada

416-361-6332, 1-888-466-6332

www.mfda.ca

Office of the Superintendent of Financial Institutions

416-973-6662, 1-800-385-8647

www.osfi-bsif.gc.ca

Ombudsman for Banking Services and Investments

416-287-2877, 1-888-451-4519

www.obsi.ca

Portfolio Management Association of Canada,

416-504-1118

www.portfoliomanagement.org

Small Investor Protection Association

416-614-9128

www.sipa.ca

Toronto Stock Exchange/TSX Venture Exchange

416-947-4670, 1-888-873-8392

www.tsx.com

Consumers should stop reading and watching investment pornography. Instead, they should focus more on the elements of their financial lives over which they have direct control—things such as cost, taxes, planning, and personal behaviour. Ask more and better questions when meeting advisors and contemplating investment products. Never buy a product that you don't totally understand. Above all, you need to realize that no one will ever care more about your finances than yourself.

No matter who you are and what your role in this story has been in the past, it wouldn't hurt to take action by contacting your local federal and provincial legislators to request immediate action on regulatory matters. Contacting premiers, ministers of finance, and the Prime Minister's Office works even better. Bringing about the continued constructive reform of the financial services industry and reinventing it as a genuine profession is everyone's business.

The transformation is well under way and will continue with or without your input. Why not take this opportunity to weigh in on enacting purposeful reforms that could literally have life-altering consequences? It is likely not an overstatement to suggest that your (and, collectively, our) financial security depends on what happens in the next few years. Every voice matters. Make sure yours is heard.

NOTES

1   Dan Wheeler, interview by Brad Steiman, 3 May 2006.

2   John Heinzl, interview by author, April 2, 2012.

3   *Projection Assumption Guidelines,* IQPF/FPSC, 2016: 9.

4   Moshe Milevsky, interview by author, March 29, 2012.

5   scientific method. Oxford Dictionaries. Oxford University Press.
    http://www.oxforddictionaries.com/definition/english/scient
    ific-method (accessed August 29, 2016).

6   Mark Carhart, "On Persistence in Mutual Fund Performance," *The Journal of Finance*, Vol. 52, No. 1, March 1997: 57–82.

7   Gary P. Brinson et al., "Determinants of Portfolio Performance," *Financial Analysts Journal*, January/February 1995: 133–138.

8   Ibid.

9   William F. Sharpe, "The Arithmetic of Active Management," *Financial Analysts Journal*, Vol. 47, No. 1, January/February 1991: 7–9.

10 Michael C. Jensen, "The Performance of Mutual Funds in the Period 1945–1964," *The Journal of Finance*, Volume 23, Issue 2, 1967: 389–416.

11 Mark Carhart, "On Persistence in Mutual Fund Performance," *The Journal of Finance*, Vol. 52, No. 1, March 1997: 57–82.

12 Robert D. Arnott et al., "How Well Have Taxable Investors Been Served in the 1980s and 1990s?" *The Journal of Portfolio Management,* Summer 2000, Vol. 26, No. 4: 84–93.

13 Larry Swedroe, "What Are the Odds of an Active Portfolio Outperforming?" CBS MoneyWatch, July 14, 2011.

14 William F. Sharpe, "The Parable of Money Managers," *Financial Analysts Journal*, Vol. 32, No. 4, July/August 1976: 4.

15   Paul A. Samuelson, "Proof That Properly Anticipated Prices Fluctuate Randomly," *Industrial Management Review*, No. 6 (Spring 1965): 41–49.

16   "Is there life after Babe Ruth? Peter Lynch talks about why he's quitting Magellan," *Barron's*, April 2, 1990: 15.

17   "Chairman's Letter," Berkshire Hathaway Inc., 1996.

18   Ibid, 2005.

19   Beverly Goodman, "A Different Dimension," *Barron's*, January 4, 2014.

20   Daniel Kahneman, *Thinking Fast and Slow,* New York: Random, 2011: 215.

21   Ibid.

22   Amin Mawani et al., "The Impact of Personal Income Taxes on Returns and Rankings of Canadian Equity Mutual Funds," *Canadian Tax Journal*, Vol. 51, No. 2, 2003: 863–901.

23   Brad Barber et al., "Out of Sight, Out of Mind: The Effects of Expenses on Mutual Fund Flows," *The Journal of Business,* Vol. 78, Issue 6, 2005: 2095–2120.

24   Russel Kinnel, "Predictive Power of Fees: Why Mutual Fund Fees Are So Important," *Morningstar*, May 4, 2016.

25   Source: The Vanguard Group Inc. This hypothetical example is for illustrative purposes only and does not represent the return of any particular investment. Assumptions include a 6% compound annual return and an initial investment of $100,000. Distributions are included, but transaction costs, bid-ask spreads, inflation, and income taxes payable by any unitholder are not included. Actual investment results will vary upward or downward, and this example does not factor in risks associated with market volatility or short-term events.

26   Ibid.

27   Rob Carrick, "New disclosure rules will bring drama to client-investor relations," *The Globe and Mail*, May 13, 2015: B11.

28   Christopher Davis, "How much are your mutual funds really costing you?" *Morningstar*, July 20, 2016.

29   Clare O'Hara, "The struggle for more transparency," *The Globe and Mail*, January 27, 2016: B12.

30 James Langton, "OSC Dialogue: Disclosure no enough to protect investors," *Investment Executive*, October 8, 2015.

31 Luke Kawa, "Vanguard, the Unlikely Savior of Active Management," *Bloomberg*, July 11, 2016.

32 Ryan Rich et al., "Putting a value on your value: Quantifying Vanguard Advisor's Alpha in Canada," Valley Forge, PA: The Vanguard Group Inc., 2015.

33 Ibid.

34 "Quantitative Analysis of Investor Behavior," DALBAR, May 2016.

35 Linnainmaa, Melzer, and Previera, "Costly Financial Advice: Conflicts of Interest or Misguided Investment Beliefs," working paper, 2015.

36 Will Ashworth, "Financial Reforms Failing? Think Again," *Wealth Professional*, November 20, 2015.

37 Michael S. Finke, "Financial Advice: Does It Make a Difference?" *Social Science Research Network*, May 5, 2012.

38 "Do Canadians Value Financial Advice?" *Advisor.ca,* November 18, 2015.

39 Stephen Foley, "Outflows accelerate from US active funds," *Financial Times*, July 18, 2016.

40 "Your Fund Manager Is Likely Overpaid," www.fund-manager.org, April 2, 2006 (accessed August 14, 2006).

41 "Risk Insurance Escapes Commission Ban," insurancenews.com.au, April 27, 2010.

42 Tessie Sanci, "U.K. reforms have an impact," *Investment Executive*, May 6, 2015.

43 Ellen Bessner, interview by author, May 1, 2012.

44 Paul Bates, interview by author, April 20, 2012.

45 James Langton, "OSC to propose introduction of 'best interest' standard," *Investment Executive*, March 10, 2016.

46 Mary Condon, "A best interest standard is needed, says a former OSC commissioner," *Investment Executive*, July 1, 2016.

47 The CFA Institute's "Statement of Investor Rights" can be found at http://www.cfainstitute.org/learning/future/getinvolved/Pages/statement_of_investor_rights.aspx.

48 "Investor Trust Study," CFA Institute & Edelman, 2013.

49 "IFIC Releases Monthly Statistics for June 2016," IFIC, July 15, 2016.

50 "Canadian ETF Assets as of May 31, 2016," Industry Statistics, CETFA.

51 Stats and Facts, IFIC. http://www.ific.ca/en/info/stats-and-facts/ (accessed September 5, 2016).

52 Tessie Sanci, "Survey: What clients want," *Investment Executive*, November 27, 2015.

53 Rudy Mezzetta, "Increasing clients' financial literacy," *Investment Executive*, December 2014: 6.

54 Janet McFarland, "High-cost fund sales fell after Britain's fee reform, regulator says," *The Globe and Mail*, October 8, 2015.

55 James Langton, "A packed agenda," *Investment Executive*, November 2014: 6.

INDEX

ABOUT THE AUTHOR

John J. De Goey, CFP, CIM, FELLOW OF FPSC™, is a portfolio manager (PM) with Industrial Alliance Securities (iAS). He enjoys a national reputation as an authority on professional, transparent, and evidence-based financial advice.

A frequent commentator on financial matters, De Goey has written for a number of media sources including *Advisor's Edge Report*, *Canadian MoneySaver*, *The Globe and Mail*, and the *National Post* and has made numerous appearances on a variety of television programs, including CBC's *Marketplace*, *News World*, and *The National*; BNN's *Market Call*; and CTV's *Canada AM*. In 2003, De Goey released his groundbreaking book, *The Professional Financial Advisor*, which was later updated and re-released in both 2006 and 2012.

De Goey is a recipient of the National Multimedia Award conferred by the Canadian Association of Financial Planners (CAFP); the past president of the CAFP's Toronto chapter; and one of only sixty-five Canadians to be recognized as a Fellow of FPSC™ for his contribution to the advancement of financial planning. In both 2014 and 2015, *Wealth Professional* magazine named him one of the top fifty advisors in Canada.

De Goey has spoken at numerous conferences throughout Canada as well as in Ireland, the US, and the Caribbean and has lectured on behalf of the Canadian Securities Institute (CSI).

His website is www.johndegoey.com. Follow him on Twitter: @JohnDeGoey_iAS.

CPSIA information can be obtained
at www.ICGtesting.com
Printed in the USA
LVOW13s2229030217
523209LV00002B/3/P

9 781554 831739